Valuation of the Liability Structure by Real Options

Modern Finance, Management Innovation and Economic Growth Set

coordinated by
Faten Ben Bouheni

Volume 5

Valuation of the Liability Structure by Real Options

David Heller

iSTE

WILEY

First published 2022 in Great Britain and the United States by ISTE Ltd and John Wiley & Sons, Inc.

ISTE Ltd
27-37 St George's Road
London SW19 4EU
UK

www.iste.co.uk

John Wiley & Sons, Inc.
111 River Street
Hoboken, NJ 07030
USA

www.wiley.com

Library of Congress Control Number: 2021950761

British Library Cataloguing-in-Publication Data
A CIP record for this book is available from the British Library
ISBN 978-1-78630-734-7

Contents

Introduction

The traditional approaches to valuating companies are currently grouped into three categories: the patrimonial method is based on the value of company assets, the multiples method consists of determining a value using similar companies as a reference or transactions that took place in the same sector, and the method of discounted cash flows tries to consider the development potential of the company. These different methods are used by those who think the value obtained by one of them should not be the focus, but rather an approach that seeks to link them. This recommendation is justified given that the practice is not an exact science.

Nevertheless, these different approaches have specific and common limits. Indeed, the multiples method can lead the analyst to false sector-specific multiples when the company reference contains large disparities in terms of financial structure or investment policy. The DCF method depends on hypotheses, which in turn depend on the analyst's subjectivity. In this way, each one can justify a level of provisional cash flow and weighted mean cost of capital by justifying the pertinence of the established business plan. The patrimonial approach counts on the value of assets in the current portfolio and excludes, as such, any potential for growth.

Otherwise, they have the common disadvantage of considering an accounting net debt rather than an economic net debt[1], and omitting the notion of flexibility with respect to investment decisions. In practice, indeterminate elements can lead a company to account for unforeseen cash

1 The net debt is the difference between the financial debt on the one hand, and the cash flow and equivalent of cash flows, on the other.

flow at the moment of investment. In order to obtain the economic value of personal equity, we subtract the value of net debt from the value of the company. But to be completely methodologically coherent, in each approach, we would have to take the economic value of the net debt into account instead.

Furthermore, these methods do not include the notion of flexibility, which is essential for any investment decision. Indeed, the unforeseen cash flows of model creation can appear while devising an investment plan. In this case, considering the total risk through the volatility of assets is something that would allow us to reach a better value.

Real options give us solutions with respect to this lack of flexibility. They are based on the concept of traditional financial options and by extension, have their utility. Thus, if real options are used for the study and valuation of an investment project (just like an NPV, or Net Present Value), we can suppose that there is a possible extension for the structure of liabilities and shareholders' equity[2].

In the case of real options, the implication is a "real" asset that has not been assessed. Because of this, the potential investment of a company can be seen as an entrance fee that allows us to access future opportunities. Thus, the value of a project is not limited to the present value of anticipated cash flow, but must capture all of the opportunities for growth that will present themselves in the future. Real options will then offer the advantage of incorporating the possibility of an increase, as well as a decrease in future cash flows through the parameter of volatility. Indeed, the incertitude is the reflection of the volatility of assets and the prospects of evolution in the project that would result in strategic decisions. The company can, for example, make the choice to abandon its project, follow through with it or extend it… This concept of flexibility is not taken into account in the NPV criteria and, thus, in the DCF method.

From this perspective, since liabilities are the mirror of company assets, its economic value and the value of its debts can also be studied with respect to options. By adopting a logic based on the sale of a company, shareholders, who have a limited responsibility with respect to creditors in a capital

2 To the extent that the economic value of assets is equal to the economic value of liabilities and shareholders' equity.

company, can recover assets from the company, as long as they pay back the nominal value of the debt. And, as in a capital company, the shareholders have a limited responsibility with regard to creditors, the economic value, which corresponds to their wealth, and is analogous to the value of the purchasing option of assets. In other words, shareholders have a claim over the assets. They can buy them as long as they reimburse the creditors. The optional references (notably Black and Scholes (1973)[3] and Merton (1974)[4]) thus propose a new company value taken from the sum of the economic value and the net debt.

The theoretical comparison between traditional methods and the real options method must extend to practical use. Whether a company's investment plan is more or less risky, and as a consequence, if the asset portfolio – and thus the liabilities structure – is more or less volatile whether the value of the net debt is bigger or smaller and whether its maturity is longer or shorter, the results from different valuation methods could very well vary and become more or less pertinent and reliable within a particular sector. Indeed, by trying to consider the economic value of net debt from an optional perspective, the analyst evaluating the economic value of a company using the Black–Scholes–Merton method could detect a potential for growth, meaning that stock prices are somewhat underestimated. In other words, in this case, the valuation of economic value results in the following estimation:

Since a company's investment portfolio value, that is, its assets, is equal to the value of its liabilities, to what extent can the approach using real options be applied to the valuation of a company's liabilities structure?

The first section will focus on the application of real options to the liabilities structure. The limits of traditional valuation methods, which the approach using options is aiming to resolve, will first be presented. Then, the optional valuation models in discrete time and continuous time will be developed, in order to locate their convergence. This theoretical framework will end in a valuation of economic value and debt using an optional approach. The second section will be dedicated to the study of the financial

3 Black, F. and Scholes, M. (1973). The pricing of options and corporate liabilities. *Journal of Political Economy*, 81(3), 637–654.

4 Merton, R.C. (1974). On the pricing of corporate debt: The risk structure of interest rates. *Journal of Finance*, 29(2), 449–470.

literature, which will specify the aspects and the stakes of economic debt and examine the adjustment of systematic risk in economic value. Then, the scientific articles that have been studied will elucidate the impact of the agency conflicts that exist between shareholders and creditors on the optional approach to the issue. Finally, debt refinancing mechanisms and their impact on economic value will be addressed. A third part will deal with two studies carried out on different dates, including statistical tests of the traditional valuation methods and following the real options approach. The first study concentrates on companies in the CAC 40 index. The second study examines companies in the cinema industry.

1

The Utility of Real Options in the Valuation of Liabilities

1.1. Introduction

Traditional valuation methods can appear overly static when faced with the need to account for the notion of the overall company risk through the volatility of its assets, as well as the need to determine the economic value of the debt, which until now, has been ignored. Indeed, insofar as the final objective of each of these valuation methods is to obtain the economic value of equity, that of net debt cannot be separated from this consideration if we take it to its logical conclusion.

Moreover, each of these traditional methods can be critiqued. The subjectivity of hypotheses in the construction of a business plan at the heart of the DCF method, the disparities at the heart of a sample set of companies belonging to the same business sector leading to falsified sector-specific multiples, and even the failure to consider any potential growth at the heart of the patrimonial approach are all faults that bias the valuation and raise the question of the pertinence of these traditional methods, suggesting the possibility that a complementary and innovative method exists.

Insofar as the assets of a company can be considered a portfolio of real options, nothing negates the idea that it would be the same for liability. And indeed, the value of company equity and debts can also be studied in the field of options.

This approach allows us to separate the equity of a company into intrinsic value and time value. The intrinsic value is the difference between the present economic value of the asset and the nominal amount of debt. The time value is the expectation that the company value will become greater than the amount of net debt to be repaid. Otherwise, the time value is zero. In this case, real options are therefore useful in valuating equity economically by distinguishing the possible creation of value for shareholders after a merger-acquisition, but they turn out to be just as necessary for economically valuating the net debt. It then turns out that the risk of debt can have an entirely different impact on the value of a company, due to the emergence of a probability of bankruptcy and the rate of non-recovery in the models.

1.2. Real options: a mitigating alternative to the deficiency of traditional valuation methods

Traditional valuation methods are subject to fundamental methodological critiques in general and in the case of each one. In each method, the volatility of assets is not accounted for and the value of net debt is counted when it should be, as with equity, economic. Furthermore, the multiples method can give the impression of large gaps in the multiples of the standard, tied in particular to significant differences in terms of marginal rates, investment politics, accounting norms used, financial structures or tax rates between companies. Thus, the sector-specific multiples used to valuate a company can be biased. An intuitive and legitimate reflex, at the end of the day, leads to the removal of elements that seem inacceptable.

Nonetheless, this reflex is subjective. If, theoretically, the DCF method is infallible in the sense that its logic brings us to the conclusion that a company is worth what it will become, the necessary parameters for the creation of a model are based on strong hypotheses that can vary considerably from one analyst to another. Finally, the patrimonial method, which remains difficult for an external analyst to apply, finds its limit in the fact that, by focusing on the patrimonial present of a company, any forecasts are voluntarily excluded.

By insisting on economically valuating the structure of liabilities, real options allow us to adopt an alternative point of view. By adopting an optional logic, it becomes possible to consider that equity is the reflection of the purchase from a call and that debt is that of a sale from a put. Thus, the Black–Scholes model (1973) is legitimized.

1.2.1. *The limits of traditional approaches*

The comparables approach must allow us to define pertinent standards. This is a complicated task, however. In order for the sample to be reliable, it must indeed be representative of the business sector and account for a certain level of risk and development related to financial performance and a similar model. Moreover, significant deviations can be seen in the fact that the chosen standards might include international companies that apply different accounting norms. To limit large disparities, it is possible to apply regressive statistical tools. This reveals a linear relationship between a valuation multiple and the principal performance criteria that affects them. In the case of transactional comparables, we must recall that a control premium was applied by the buyer.

It is therefore necessary to subtract value in order to correct this effect. Traditionally, practitioners begin with a large standard that becomes smaller over time to maintain companies or "satisfying" transactions, with respect to the different points raised here. Otherwise, the major inconvenience of the patrimonial approach is that it does not consider the growth potential of a company. In the DCF approach[1], the company value (or enterprise value, *EV*) is the discounted value of future free cash flows *FCF*, the discount rate being the weighted mean cost of capital or WACC *K*:

$$\mathrm{EV} = \sum_{t=1}^{+\infty} \frac{\mathrm{FCF_t}}{(1+\mathrm{K})^t} \text{ with } \mathrm{K} = \mathrm{k}\frac{\mathrm{E}}{\mathrm{E+D}} + \mathrm{i}(1-\tau)\frac{\mathrm{D}}{\mathrm{E+D}} \qquad [1.1]$$

where *E* is the value of equity and *D* is the net debt. The WACC contained in the calculation of the company value is based on the equity value, which is found using the DCF method. It is the reason why practitioners include an iterative life cycle in their approach. By supposing an infinite rate of growth of FCF *g* starting at year 1 and a WACC equal to *K*:

$$\mathrm{EV} = \frac{\mathrm{FCF}(1+\mathrm{g})}{\mathrm{K-g}} \text{ and } \mathrm{K} = \mathrm{k}\frac{\mathrm{E}}{\mathrm{EV}} + \mathrm{i}(1-\tau)\frac{\mathrm{D}}{\mathrm{EV}} \qquad [1.2]$$

1 Heller, D. and Levyne, O. (2014). Is the growth potential of stock prices underestimated? *International Journal of Business*, 19(4), 336–360.

By referring to the cost of capital adjusted by Modigliani and Miller (1963), we can eliminate the life cycle. Indeed, $K = \rho.\left(1 - \frac{D.\tau}{EV}\right)$, where ρ is the cost of capital for a debtless company with the same sector-specific rate risk. In other words, thanks to the CAPM, $\rho = r + \beta^{*}[E(R_M) - r]$, where r is the rate without risk. Thus:

$$\mathrm{EV} = \frac{\mathrm{FCF}(1+\mathrm{g})}{\rho.\left(1-\frac{D.\tau}{EV}\right)-\mathrm{g}} \text{ and } \mathrm{EV} = \frac{\mathrm{FCF}(1+\mathrm{g})+\mathrm{D}.\tau.\rho}{\rho-\mathrm{g}} \qquad [1.3]$$

where $D\tau$ is the tax rate that results from fiscal deductibility of interest to the extent that we suppose an infinite net debt. Indeed, in the Modigliani–Miller theory, $D\tau$ comes from the simplification of $\frac{i.D.\tau}{i}$, where $iD\tau$ is the interest tax economy and i is the corresponding tax rate. In this case, D is obviously the remaining debt owed, found in the latest available financial statements. When practitioners deduct D from EV to obtain the value of equity, the following formula E is obtained:

$$\mathrm{E} = \frac{\mathrm{FCF}.(1+\mathrm{g})+\mathrm{D}.[\mathrm{g}-\rho.(1-\tau)]}{\rho-\mathrm{g}} \qquad [1.4]$$

The Modigliani–Miller theory shows that the strike price on risky debt has no impact on the WACC, and, as a result of this, it has no impact on the value of equity: the cost of debt does not appear in the two previous formulas, and a rise in the strike price of the debt corresponds to a rise in the risk that can be tolerated by the investors and banks. It is therefore logical that a drop in risk is tolerated by shareholders. For a simple example, Table 1.1 shows that the transfer of risk between shareholders and investors does not change the value of the WACC.

With an FCF equal to 100, a risk-free rate of 2%, a market risk premium of 7% and a debtless *beta* of 0.9, two hypotheses about the cost of debt before taxes arise: 3.40%, based on a debt *beta* of 0.20, and 5.50%, based on a debt *beta* of 0.50. The corresponding indebted *betas*, based on the Hamada formula, are, respectively, 1.18 and 1.06, and the deducted equity costs are 10.27% and 9.43%, respectively. Thus, the two WACC and adjusted capital costs are 7.06%. Finally, the company value is the same in both cases: 2,538.

FCF	100	100
Infinite growth rate = g	3.00%	300%
Risk-free rate = r	2.00%	2.00%
Market risk premium	7.00%	7.00%
Debtless beta = β*	0.90	0.90
Cost of the debt		
Cost of the debt before taxes	3.40%	5.50%
After taxes with an IS rate of 38%	2.11%	3.41%
Beta of the debt	0.20	0.5
Indebted beta = β	1.18	1.06
Cost of equity = k	10.27%	9.43%
WACC = K	7/06%	7.06%
ρ	8.30%	8.30%
Adjusted cost of capital	7.06%	7.06%
EV	2,538	2,538
Debt	1,000	1,000
Equity	1,538	1,538

Table 1.1. *Transfer of risk between shareholders and investors without impacting the WACC using the DCF approach*[2]

The calculation of the WACC is "subjective" given the numerous hypotheses to take into account:

– the market risk premium depends on a hypothesis concerning the infinite growth rate of dividends for listed companies;

– when the company is listed, the cost of capital can include either a *beta* (different depending on who provides the data) or an indebted *beta* based on a debtless industrial *beta*, which relies on the creation of a sample pair for the company that is to be valuated;

– the weighted coefficients can correspond to the target financial structure, or be based on an iterative calculation. Thus, the equity value is the result of a valuation obtained via DCF.

In other words, each broker can justify their own discount rate.

2 Heller, D. (2018). Valorisation d'entreprise : méthodes traditionnelles et approche innovante par les options réelles. In *Tradition et innovation : de l'opposition à la complémentarité*, Anido Freire, N. (ed.). L'Harmattan, Paris.

The value of equity, moreover, is the difference between the value of the company *EV* and the net debt *D*. The net debt is the difference between the financial debt, on the one hand, and the cash flow and equivalents of cash flow, on the other. The maturity of the debt is not taken into account. So, if the *EV* is 100 and the financial debt is 60, supposing there is no cash flow nor any equivalents of cash flow, the value of equity will be 40, whether the debt reaches maturity tomorrow or in 2023.

The reason is because practitioners generally take the face value of the debt into account (without a reimbursement premium) instead of taking the economic value of the debt into account, even though the financial theory depends on the economic values of stocks, which are supplied by the shareholders of companies. If the debt reaches maturity tomorrow, its economic value corresponds to its face value, but if it reaches maturity in 2023, its economic value corresponds to the present value of cash flows expected by investors, with the discount rate reflecting the company's risk of bankruptcy. In other words, the company's risk of bankruptcy is not tied to the debt that is deducted from the company value and it is included in the weighted coefficients of the WACC.

Finally, the DCF method is based on FCF, which are implicitly considered determinants. They are discounted, which allows us to reduce their weight in the company value. Since the cost of equity, accounted for in the WACC, is based on the CAPM, the reference to the indebted beta of companies allows us to incorporate systemic risk. Moreover, an analysis of sensibility is generally accomplished by practitioners, in order to underscore the lack of certainty in creating business plans. Nevertheless, the risk, that is, the total volatility (σ) of FCF, is not taken into account.

The innovative approach of real options notably provides solutions by considering the economic value of a net debt, and by combining the strategic flexibility of an investment with its irreversible character[3] and the risks that are associated with it. For any given level of irreversibility in an investment, the value of real options tied to a project will depend on the risk and managerial flexibility. Managers can then proceed to alternative choices in their management of the investment or when competing advantages allow them to wait before investing.

3 Once completed, an investment generates an irrecuperable cost.

1.2.2. *The alternative of real options*

Financial options are meant to be used in speculative strategies, hedging and/or arbitration concerning an underlying asset. We have the right to call or put a financial asset on a given date (option in the European sense) or during a given period (option in the American sense) at a known price called the strike price. To become the owner of a financial option, we must pay a premium. The latter depends on the value of the underlying asset S, the strike price E, the remaining maturity before the due date τ, the volatility of the underlying asset σ and the risk-free rate r.

As for the premium, it includes an intrinsic value and a time value. The time value is the value complement beyond the intrinsic value, which indicates the expectation of a favorable evolution in the price of the asset between now and the deadline for the option. Insofar as the expectation is zero at maturity, the time value is also zero. The intrinsic value corresponds to the value of the option at a particular moment. For a call, the intrinsic value is equal to the *max* (*S-E; 0*). For a put, the intrinsic value is equal to the *max* (*S-E; 0*).

In the case of speculative strategies, the call must reflect the buyer's (seller's) expectations of an increase (decrease) in the underlying cost. Inversely, the put must reflect the buyer's (seller's) expectations of a decrease (increase) in the underlying cost. Supposing a premium of 10 € and a strike price of 100, we have the following graphs for each scenario.

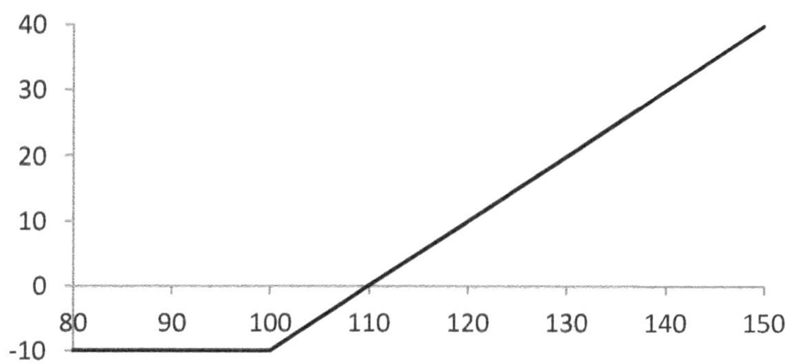

Figure 1.1. *Purchase of a call*

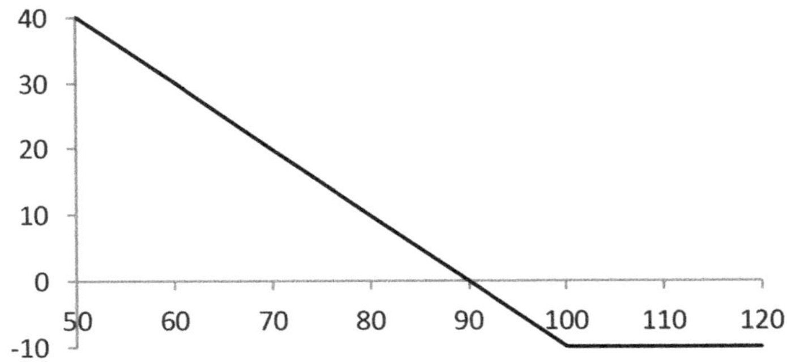

Figure 1.2. *Purchase of a put*

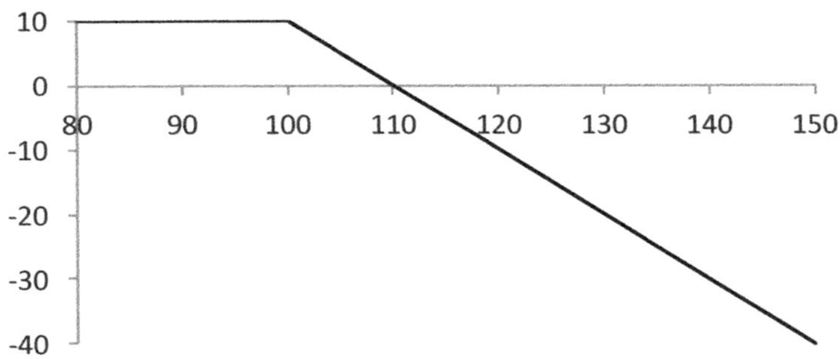

Figure 1.3. *Sale of a call*

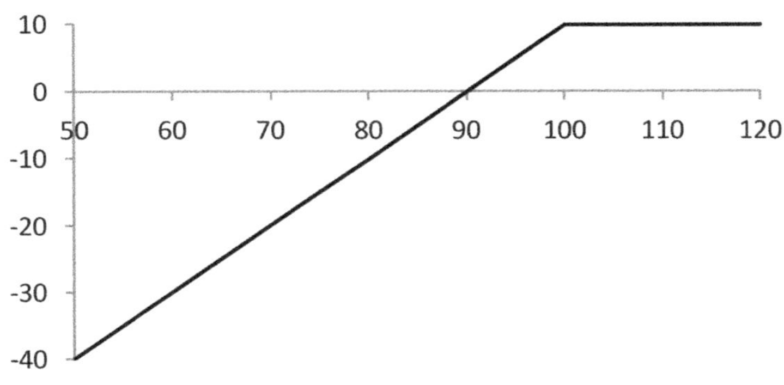

Figure 1.4. *Sale of a put*

The values of the underlying asset are on the horizontal axis; the gains and losses figure is on the vertical axis. The figures can be analyzed as such:

– in the case of the purchase of a call, the perspective for losses is limited to the premium paid (10 €), while the perspective for gains becomes greater as the price of the asset rises;

– in the case of the purchase of a put, the perspective for losses is limited to the premium paid (10 €), while the perspective for gains becomes greater as the price of the asset falls. It is a speculation strategy on the fall in price of the asset;

– in the case of the sale of a call, the perspective for gains is limited to the premium received (10 €), while the perspective for losses becomes greater as the price of the asset rises. This is a speculation strategy on the fall in price of the asset and is riskier, with lower perspectives for gains than in the case of the purchase of a put. This strategy is recommended by a speculator of losses without liquidity;

– in the case of the sale of a put, the perspective for gains is limited to the premium received (10 €), while the perspective for losses becomes greater as the price of the asset falls. This is a riskier speculation strategy on the rise of the price of the asset, with lower perspectives for gains than in the case of the purchase of a call. This strategy is recommended by a speculator of gains without liquidity.

The essential legal principle of an anonymous company is the limitation on shareholder responsibility with respect to creditors. Indeed, when a company goes bankrupt, shareholders can abandon the company to its creditors. In this context, shareholders can lose the entirety of their contributions while their gains are illimited, as long as the company generates value. Here, we see the foundation of an analogy with financial options: shareholders have a purchase option (call) over the company.

This option is not financial but “real” because the underlying asset is not financial security, such as a share or bond, but the value of the company, that is, its investment portfolio; the strike price being the amount of borrowed debt; the maturity corresponding to the duration of debt and the volatility to that of the economic asset. Since at the maturity of the debt, shareholders decide whether or not to use their purchasing option and pay off the creditors, the value (premium) of the option therefore corresponds to the economic value of equity.

Inversely, it is possible to consider that creditors may have sold a "real" European sale option (put) over the value of the company; the strike price being the amount of loaned debt; the maturity corresponding to the duration of the loan and the volatility to that of the underlying economic asset. Indeed, their loan comes down to the fact that they invested in the riskless asset and sold a put over the economic asset to the shareholders; the strike price is the amount of borrowed debt. From this, if the company does not manage to repay its loan, the creditors recover the economic asset "purchased in spite of them" for the amount of the unreimbursed debt. Consequently, it seems legitimate for the creditor to add an interest rate superior to the risk-free rate in order to pay themselves. Indeed, by following the logic of options, the creditor runs the risk of the put being opted for by the shareholders, that is, the company would not reimburse the borrowed amount.

There is therefore a fundamental asymmetry between the status of the shareholder described previously and that of the creditor. The latter recovers the contractually expected fluctuations, at best. In other words, even if the required rate of return is identical for a shareholder and a creditor, their respective notions are fundamentally different: for the shareholder, this rate is closer to the expectation of gains, while from the creditor's point of view, the rate has a very high probability of being reached and can, by no means, be surpassed.

Having established an analogy between the structure of liabilities and options, it would be interesting to develop the optional valuation models.

1.2.3. *Black–Scholes optional modeling*

Optional modeling began with Black and Scholes (1973)[4]. Their model in continuous time follows the principle of log-normalization of the underlying asset price. The latter defines a Brownian geometric motion:

$$dS = \mu S dt + \rho S dz \quad [1.5]$$

4 Black, F. and Scholes, M. (1973). The pricing of options and corporate liabilities. *Journal of Political Economy*, 81(3), 637–654.

where:

– μ: expected return of the share (obtained using the CAPM);

– σ: volatility of the share;

– $dz = \varepsilon\, dt$ with ε following a normal distribution.

The Ito lemma allows us to calculate the premium of the call:

$$dC(S;t) = \left[\frac{\partial C}{\partial t} + \frac{\partial C}{\partial S}\mu S + S^2.\sigma^2 \frac{1}{2}\frac{\partial^2 C}{\partial S^2}\right]dt + \sigma S\frac{\partial C}{\partial S}dz \qquad [1.6]$$

The Black–Scholes formula starts with the creation of a risk-free arbitration portfolio. Supposing that the values of dz are identical for the option and for the underlying asset, insofar as only the term $\sigma S\,\frac{\partial C}{\partial S}\,dz$ has a random variable, the portfolio will not have risk if the terms in dz compensate for each other. The portfolio P is thus made of a sold option and $\frac{\partial C}{\partial S}$ purchased shares:

$$P = -C + \frac{\partial C}{\partial S}.S \qquad [1.7]$$

and:

$$dP = -dC + \frac{\partial C}{\partial S}\,.dS \qquad [1.8]$$

$$= -\left[\frac{\partial C}{\partial t} + \frac{\partial C}{\partial S}\mu S + \frac{1}{2}S^2.\sigma^2\frac{\partial^2 C}{\partial S^2}\right]dt - \sigma S\frac{\partial C}{\partial S}dz + \frac{\partial C}{\partial S}[\mu S.dt + \sigma S.dz] \qquad [1.9]$$

By simplifying with $\mu S.\frac{\partial C}{\partial S}\,dt$ and $\sigma S\frac{\partial C}{\partial S}\,dz$, we have:

$$dP = \left[-\frac{\partial C}{\partial t} - \frac{1}{2}S^2.\sigma^2\frac{\partial^2 C}{\partial S^2}\right]dt \qquad [1.10]$$

This risk-free portfolio gives the return r, homogeneous with dt. Thus:

$$\left[-\frac{\partial C}{\partial t} - \frac{1}{2}S^2.\sigma^2\frac{\partial^2 C}{\partial S^2}\right]dt = \left[-C + \frac{\partial C}{\partial S}.S\right]r.dt \qquad [1.11]$$

By simplifying with dt:

$$\left[-\frac{\partial C}{\partial t} - \frac{1}{2}S^2.\sigma^2\frac{\partial^2 C}{\partial S^2}\right] = \left[-C + \frac{\partial C}{\partial S}.S\right]r \qquad [1.12]$$

Thus:

$$\frac{\partial C}{\partial t} + r.S\frac{\partial C}{\partial S} + \frac{1}{2}S^2.\sigma^2\frac{\partial^2 C}{\partial S^2} = r.C \qquad [1.13]$$

By extending the reasoning, convergence points between the different fundamental models can be found. In this context, the equity, as well as the debt can be economically valuated.

1.3. Intersections between approaches to assets valuation

The Black–Scholes (1973) and Cox–Ross–Rubinstein (1979)[5] models can converge. Merton (1973)[6] refines this type of approach by integrating the notion of dividend payout. By having the CAPM and the Modigliani–Miller theory converge in the absence of any fiscality, followed by the Black–Scholes model with this same theory, it turns out that, in accordance with Modigliani and Miller's conclusion, the cost of capital is equal to that of a company's debt-free equity and presents the same industry risk. Thus, the consideration of the economic value of debt reveals its full importance.

1.3.1. *Convergence between the Cox–Ross–Rubinstein (1979) and the Black–Scholes (1973) models and the Merton formula (1973)*

The Cox–Ross–Rubenstein model (1979) supposes that the value of the underlying asset follows a binomial multiplication principle for discrete time. At the end of the first period, the underlying asset can indeed grow (uS) with the probability q or decrease (dS)[7] with l-q. If the value of the asset grows (or decreases), the premium of the call also grows (or decreases) with the probability q (or with the probability l-q).

5 Cox, J., Ross, S., Rubinstein, M. (1979). Options pricing: A simplified approach. *Journal of Financial Economics*, 7(3), 229–263.

6 Merton, R.C. (1973). Theory of rational option pricing. *Bell Journal of Economics*, 4(1), 141–183.

7 u for *upward* and d for *downward*.

After creating a hedge portfolio *P* made up of the purchase of a call with the premium *C* and the sale of *H* shares, we have:

$$C = \frac{1}{\hat{r}}.\,[p.\,C_u + (1-p)C_d],\ \text{where}\ p = q = \frac{\hat{r}-d}{u-d}\ \text{and}\ \hat{r} = (1+r)^{\tau} \qquad [1.14]$$

After taking a discount rate in continuous time:

$$C = e^{-r'\tau}.\,E[\max(S_t - E), 0] \qquad [1.15]$$

where S_t is the value of the underlying asset at maturity.

If *a* corresponds to the minimal number of upward movements of the asset over the next *n* periods, such that the call is "in the money" and will be exercised, and if *F (a,n,p)* is related to the binomial distribution function inherent to the probability that allows the call to be exercised at maturity, we have:

$$C = SF(a, n, p') - E\hat{r}^{-n}F(a, n, p) \qquad [1.16]$$

Cox and Rubenstein (1985)[8] show that when the number of periods between the evaluation date and the maturity date of the option tend towards infinity, their formula converges towards that of Black–Scholes. Indeed, if *n* is very high, the binomial multiplication principle of the price of the asset follows a normal log distribution and:

$$C = S\Phi(d_1) - Ee^{-r\tau}\Phi(d_2) \qquad [1.17]$$

with:

$$d_1 = \frac{\ln\left(\frac{S}{E}\right)+\left(r'+\frac{\sigma^2}{2}\right)\tau}{\sigma\sqrt{\tau}} \qquad [1.18]$$

$$d_2 = d_1 - \sigma\sqrt{\tau} \qquad [1.19]$$

$$\Phi(x) = \frac{1}{\sqrt{2\pi}}\int_{-\infty}^{x} e^{-\frac{r^2}{2}}dt \qquad [1.20]$$

8 Cox, J. and Rubinstein, M. (1985). *Options Markets*. Prentice Hall, Englewood Cliffs, NJ.

where:

– S: spot of the underlying share;

– E: strike (exercise price) of the option;

– τ: time to maturity (in years);

– r: discrete risk-free rate;

– r': continuous risk-free rate, with: $r' = ln(1+r)$;

– σ: volatility of the underlying asset;

– $\Phi(.)$: normal distribution function;

– $\Phi(d_2)$ replaces $F(a,n,p)$ and corresponds to the probability that the *call* will be exercised at maturity.

Merton (1973)[9] allows for a payout of dividends in continuous time at the annualized rate q[10]. If a dividend distribution is made between the dates $t = 0$ and $t = T$, the price of the asset S is replaced by $S\ T.\ e^{qt}$. The effect of the distribution of dividends is then integrated in the Black–Scholes formula by replacing S by $S.\ e\text{-}^{qt}$:

$$C = S.e^{-qt}.\Phi(d_1) - Ee^{-rt}.\Phi(d_2) \quad [1.21]$$

The analogy between financial options and real options leads us to consider the parameters in Table 1.2.

Equity in terms of real options	Financial purchase options	Variable
Value of the economic asset	Price of the underlying asset	S
Total debt to be paid (economic value)	Exercise price of the option	E
Maturity of the debt	Remaining time until the option reaches maturity	τ
Time value of the money	Risk-free rate	R
Volatility of the underlying asset or even of the economic asset	Volatility (standard deviation) of the financial asset's returns	σ

Table 1.2. *Analogy between the parameters of real options with reference to liabilities structure and the parameters of the financial option*

9 Merton, R.C. (1973). Theory of rational option pricing. *Bell Journal of Economics*, 4(1), 141–183.

10 If a is the observed discrete return rate, then $q = \ln(1 + a)$.

From this, we arrive at the fundamental mechanisms listed in Table 1.3.

The dynamics of value	Impact on the economic value of equity, similar to the purchase of a call	Impact on the economic value of debt, similar to the sale of a put
Economic asset increase	Increases	Diminishes
Financial debt increase	Diminishes	Increases
Debt maturity increase	Increases	Increases
Underlying asset volatility increase	Increases	Increases
Risk-free rate increase	Increases	Diminishes
Dividend increase	Diminishes	Increases

Table 1.3. *Mechanisms impacting the value of financial structure via the real options approach*

1.3.2. Convergence between the CAPM and the Modigliani–Miller theory

In the absence of taxation, two companies should be considered identical in terms of business sector, assets and earnings before interest and taxes, but not from the perspective of financial structure: one company has debt, the other does not. The notations used in the following formulas are:

– V: the company value of an indebted company;

– V^*: the company value of a debtless company;

– R_i: share performance for the indebted company;

– R^*_i: share performance for a debtless company;

– R_M: market performance;

– β_i: market volatility of the indebted company share;

– β^*_i: market volatility of the debtless company share;

– REX: gross earnings of each of the two companies;

– D: net debt of the indebted company;

– E: equity of the indebted company;

– E^*: equity of the debtless company;

– r: risk-free rate with which we suppose it is possible to enter debt.

According to the formula for the securities market line derived from CAPM on the one hand, and the notion of equity profitability that comes from financial analysis on the other, we have:

$$E(R_i) = \frac{E(REX)-rD}{E} = r + \beta_i[E[R_M] - r] \qquad [1.22]$$

$$E(R^*_i) = \frac{E(REX)-rD}{E^*} = \frac{E(REX)}{V^*} = r + \beta^*_i[E[R_M] - r] \qquad [1.23]$$

Now, it is assumed that the two companies have the same assets, $V = V^*$. In this case, the second equation is written as:

$$E(R^*_i) = \frac{E(REX)}{V} = r + \beta^*_i[E[R_M] - r] \qquad [1.24]$$

By isolating $E[R_M] - r$ in the expressions $E(R_i)$ and $E(R^*_i)$, we get:

$$[E[R_M] - r] = \frac{E[R_i]-r}{\beta_i} = \frac{E[R^*_i]-r}{\beta^*_i} \text{ therefore } \beta_i = \beta^*_i \frac{E[R_i]-r}{E[R^*_i]-r} \qquad [1.25]$$

By returning to the definition of earnings expectations:

$$\beta_i = \beta^*_i \frac{\frac{E(REX)-rD}{E}-r}{\frac{E(REX)}{V}-r} = \beta^*_i \frac{\frac{E(REX)-rD-rE}{E}}{\frac{E(REX)-rV}{V}} \qquad [1.26]$$

or still yet:

$$\beta_i = \beta^*_i \frac{\frac{E(REX)-r(E+D)}{E}}{\frac{E(REX)-r(E+D)}{V}} = \beta^*_i \frac{\frac{1}{E}}{\frac{1}{V}} = \beta^*_i \frac{V}{E} = \beta^*_i \frac{E+D}{E} \qquad [1.27]$$

Finally:

$$\beta_i = \beta^*_i \left(1 + \frac{D}{E}\right) \qquad [1.28]$$

In this way, we arrive at the formula for the *beta* in terms of the debt-free *beta* in the absence of taxation. By reintroducing this result in the formula for the security market line, we have:

$$E(R_i) = r + \beta_i[E[R_M] - r] = r + \beta^*_i \left(1 + \frac{D}{E}\right) [E[R_M] - r] \qquad [1.29]$$

$$E(R_i) = r + \beta^*{}_i[E[R_M] - r] + \beta^*{}_i[E[R_M] - r]\frac{D}{E} \quad [1.30]$$

$$E(R_i) = E(R^*{}_i) + [E[R^*{}_i] - r]\frac{D}{E} \quad [1.31]$$

The only thing left to do is to point out, like Modigliani and Miller, that $E(R^*{}_i) = \rho$. In this case:

$$E(R_i) = \rho + [\rho - r]\frac{D}{E} \quad [1.32]$$

In the presence of taxation, that is, the tax rate *t* on companies:

$$E(R_i) = \frac{[E(REX) - rD](1-t)}{E} = r + \beta_i[E(R_M) - r] = r + \frac{cov(R_i, R_M)}{V(R_M)}[E(R_M) - r] \quad [1.33]$$

$$E(R^*{}_i) = \frac{[E(REX)](1-t)}{V^*} = r + \beta^*{}_i[E(R_M) - r] = r + \frac{cov(R^*{}_i, R_M)}{V(R_M)}[E(R_M) - r] \quad [1.34]$$

Or

$$\lambda = \frac{E(R_M) - r}{V(R_M)}$$

Then:

$$E(R_i) = \frac{[E(REX) - rD](1-t)}{E} = r + \lambda.\,cov(R_i, R_M) \quad [1.35]$$

$$E(R^*{}_i) = \frac{[E(REX)](1-t)}{V^*} = r + \lambda.\,cov(R^*{}_i, R_M) \quad [1.36]$$

Using the first equivalence:

$$\frac{[E(REX) - rD](1-t)}{E} = r + \lambda.\,cov\left[\frac{(REX - rD)(1-t)}{E}, R_M\right] \quad [1.37]$$

$$\frac{[E(REX)(1-t)]}{E} - r(1-t)\frac{D}{E} = r + \lambda(1-t)\frac{1}{E}.\,cov[REX, R_M] \quad [1.38]$$

with REX and R_M being the only random variables in the covariance. From there, by multiplying each element in the equivalence by E:

$$E(REX)(1-t) = rE + r(1-t)D + \lambda(1-t).\operatorname{cov}[REX, R_M] \qquad [1.39]$$

And using the second equivalence:

$$\frac{[E(REX)](1-t)}{V^*} = r + \lambda.\operatorname{cov}\left[\frac{REX(1-t)}{V^*}, R_M\right] \qquad [1.40]$$

$$\frac{[E(REX)](1-t)}{V^*} = r + \lambda(1-t).\frac{1}{V^*}\operatorname{cov}[REX, R_M] \qquad [1.41]$$

From there, multiplying each element in the equivalence by V^*:

$$[E(REX)](1-t) = rV^* + \lambda(1-t).\operatorname{cov}[REX, R_M] \qquad [1.42]$$

And combining the equivalences [1.39] and [1.42], we get:

$$rE + r(1-t)D + \lambda(1-t).\operatorname{cov}[REX, R_M] = rV^* + \lambda(1-t).\operatorname{cov}[REX, R_M] \qquad [1.43]$$

Or finally, by simplifying with $\lambda(1-t).cov[REX, R_M]$ and r:

$$E + D - Dt = V^* \qquad [1.44]$$

$$\text{or even: } V = V^* + Dt \qquad [1.45]$$

which indeed corresponds to the Modigliani–Miller formula in the presence of taxation.

1.3.3. *Convergence between the Black–Scholes model and the Modigliani–Miller theory outside of taxation*

We consider the hypothesis at the base of the Black–Scholes model, that is, a share whose return defines a Brownian motion with a trend.

So:

– S = value of a share, similar to a call on the company assets with a value V, and whose exercise price is the amount of net debt to repay;

– μ = instant drift;

– σ = instant volatility.

S is a function of V and the time left to maturity.

From there:

$$\frac{dS}{S} = \mu dt + \sigma dz, \text{where } dz = \varepsilon\sqrt{dt} \text{ et } \varepsilon \rightarrow N(0,1) \quad [1.46]$$

And according to the Ito lemma:

$$dS = \frac{\partial S}{\partial t}dt + \frac{\partial S}{\partial V}dV + \frac{1}{2}\frac{\partial^2 S}{\partial V^2}\sigma^2 dt,$$

which tends towards $\frac{\partial S}{\partial V}dV$ when dt tends towards 0 [1.47]

We then have:

$$\frac{dS}{S} = \frac{\partial S}{\partial V}dV.\frac{1}{S} = \frac{\partial S}{\partial V}\frac{dV}{V}.\frac{V}{S} \quad [1.48]$$

Now, $\partial S/\partial V$ represents the variation in the price of the share, that is, the premium of the option on the company assets with respect to the underlying assets. It is therefore a delta that, according to the Black–Scholes model, corresponds to $\Phi d1$.

In this case:

$$\frac{dS}{S} = \Phi(d_1)\frac{dV}{V}.\frac{V}{S} = \Phi(d_1).\rho\frac{V}{S} \quad [1.49]$$

where ρ corresponds to the profitability of the asset (return on indebted company equity) and *dS/S* corresponds to the return on indebted company shares, written from here on out as R_i.

This expression allows us to obtain β_i:

$$\beta_i = \frac{cov(R_i,R_M)}{V(R_M)} = \frac{cov\left(\Phi(d_1).\rho\frac{V}{S},R_M\right)}{V(R_M)} = \Phi(d_1).\frac{V}{S}\frac{cov(\rho,R_M)}{V(R_M)} \quad [1.50]$$

Finally:

$$\beta i = \beta * i \Phi d1VS \quad [1.51]$$

By returning to the securities market line formula, it is possible to calculate the cost of equity for an indebted company:

$$k = E(R_i) = r_f + \beta_i\left[E[R_M] - r_f\right] = r_f + \beta^*{}_i\Phi(d_1)\frac{V}{S}\left[E[R_M] - r_f\right] \quad [1.52]$$

Moreover, the securities market line formula applied to a debt-free company allows us to arrive at the expression for $\beta^*{}_i$.

$$\rho = E(R^*{}_i) = r_f + \beta^*{}_i[E[R_M] - r_f] \text{ therefore } \beta^*{}_i = \frac{\rho - r_f}{E[R_M] - r_f} \quad [1.53]$$

By replacing the value that was just obtained for $\beta^*{}_i$ in the expression of the cost of equity for the indebted company, we arrive at the conclusion that:

$$k = E(R_i) = r_f + \frac{\rho - r_f}{E[R_M] - r_f}\,\Phi(d_1)\frac{V}{S}\left[E[R_M] - r_f\right] \quad [1.54]$$

Finally:

$$k = r_f + \Phi(d_1)\frac{V}{S}(\rho - r_f) \quad [1.55]$$

It is possible to express the cost of the debt according to the same approach by starting with the beta of the debt, written β_D. It has been established that, when *dt* tends towards 0:

$$\frac{dS}{S} = \frac{\partial S}{\partial V}\frac{dV}{V}.\frac{V}{S} \quad [1.56]$$

Then, by replacing *S* with *D*:

$$\frac{dD}{D} = \frac{\partial D}{\partial D}\frac{dV}{V}.\frac{V}{S} = \frac{\partial D}{\partial V}.\rho\frac{V}{D} = i \quad [1.57]$$

Now

$$D = V - S = V - [V\Phi(d_1) - Ee^{-r_f\tau}.\Phi(d_2)] \text{ with } d_2 = d_1 - \sigma\sqrt{\tau} \quad [1.58]$$

As a result:

$$\frac{\partial D}{\partial V} = 1 - \Phi(d_1) \qquad [1.59]$$

Then:

$$i = [1 - \Phi(d_1)].\rho\frac{V}{D} \qquad [1.60]$$

Since

$$\beta_D = \frac{cov(r,R_M)}{V(R_M)} = [1 - \Phi(d_1)].\frac{V}{D}\frac{cov(\rho,R_M)}{V(R_M)} \qquad [1.61]$$

We conclude that

$$\beta_D = [1 - \Phi(d_1)].\frac{V}{D}\beta^*{}_i \qquad [1.62]$$

and according to the formula for the securities market line applied to the cost of the risky debt, written *i*:

$$i = r_f + \beta_D\big[E[R_M - r_f]\big] = r_f + [1 - \Phi(d_1)].\frac{V}{D}\beta^*{}_i\big[E[R_M - r_f]\big] \qquad [1.63]$$

and since it has been established that:

$$\beta^*{}_i = \frac{\rho - r_f}{E[R_M] - r_f} \qquad [1.64]$$

we arrive at:

$$i = r_f + [1 - \Phi(d_1)].\frac{V}{D}\frac{\rho - r_f}{E[R_M] - r_f}\big[E[R_M - r_f]\big] =$$
$$r_f + [1 - \Phi(d_1)].\frac{V}{D}(\rho - r_f) \qquad [1.65]$$

In order to get the desired convergence, we must apply the formula for the mean cost offset of capital:

$$K = k.\frac{S}{V} + i\frac{D}{V} =$$
$$\left[r_f + \Phi(d_1)\frac{V}{S}(\rho - r_f)\right]\frac{S}{V} + \left[r_f + [1 - \Phi(d_1)].\frac{V}{D}(\rho - r_f)\frac{D}{V}\right] \qquad [1.66]$$

or even

$$K = r_f.\frac{S}{V} + r_f\frac{D}{V} + (\rho - r_f) = r_f + (\rho - r_f) = \rho \qquad [1.67]$$

In this way, we have established that in the absence of taxation, the cost of capital corresponds to the cost of debt-free company equity (which presents the same industry risk), which is what the first proposition in Modigliani and Miller (1963) states.

The convergence between optional models and the theory of financial structure imagined by Modigliani and Miller lead us to examine the optional mechanisms that exist in the reduction of risky debt.

1.4. Valuation of liabilities structures with real options

The mechanisms that allow us to understand the repercussions of the value of real options on the structure of liabilities enable us to valorize the company value and produce a probability of bankruptcy and, from this, the stakes implied by the existence of risky debt.

1.4.1. *The economic value of equity and net debt*

Insofar as the balance of statements requires equality between assets and liabilities, the company value must be equal to the sum of equity capital and financial debt. Let us consider a company via shares that has only produced one type of debt (zero-coupons), payable at maturity in one lump sum (capital and interest). Depending on the economic asset value at the time of maturity, two cases can occur:

– if the economic asset value is greater than the amount of debt to be repaid, shareholders will allow the company to repay creditors and recover any residual value. In this case, the value of shareholders' call is positive, the value of the put of creditors is zero and the value of equity has a positive value (corresponding to the value of the call over economic assets);

– if the value of economic assets is less than the amount of debt to be repaid, shareholders will invoke the clause of limited risk to their contributions, lose only their contributions and abandon the economic assets to the creditors. The latter will in turn take on the difference between the value of the economic asset and the amount of their debt. In this case, the value of the shareholder call is zero, the value of the creditor put is positive and the equity no longer has value.

Present value of debt as a risk-free rate

– Value of the put on the economic asset

= Value of debts [1.68]

Value of the call

– Value of the put

+ Value of the debt at a risk-free rate

= Value of the economic assets [1.69]

Now:

Purchasing a call

+ Selling a put

= Purchasing the underlying asset + Acquiring debt at a risk-free rate [1.70]

From this:

Value of the economic assets

– Present value of the debt at the risk-free rate

+ Value of the put on the economic assets

= Value of equity [1.71]

Equity can be considered a residual claim for shareholders, since they have a claim to any cash flow remaining in the company once it has honored its financial obligations with its investors (financial debt, priority shares, etc.). Thus, from the perspective of liquidity, shareholders receive the money left over in the company once all company debts are paid off.

Nevertheless, the principle of "limited responsibility" protects shareholders in companies listed in the stock market if the value of the company is less than the value of the outstanding debt. In this case, the investors take control of the company and the shareholders receive nothing. In other words, the value of equity from the perspective of liquidity, or in the presence of a maturity date for the debt is equal to: *max* (*EV-D*;0).

The value of debts is then repaid by equity that depends on the value of the company. The latter can be considered an underlying asset since its value changes over time in an unpredictable way. The value of equity is therefore the premium of a call with the following parameters:

– *S*: the spot for the underlying asset, that is, the EV on the evaluation date;

– *E*: the exercise price, that is, the debt to be repaid at maturity;

– σ: volatility of the underlying asset, that is, the volatility of EV;

– *r*: risk-free rate;

– τ: maturity.

The probability that the call will be exercised at maturity is $\Phi(d_2)$, which corresponds to the probability that the debt will be repaid at maturity. $\Phi(d_2)$ is therefore the probability that the company will be "*in bonis*" at maturity. Thus, the probability that the debt will not be repaid because the value of the company is less than *D* (which means the company will go bankrupt) is $1 - \Phi(d_2) = \Phi(-d_2)$.

Let us suppose that the *EV* of a company is 800 when it has to repay a zero-coupon for an amount of 1,000. If the debt reaches maturity tomorrow, the probability of finding 1,000 for tomorrow is zero and the company will go bankrupt. The value of its equity is zero since the shareholders abandon the company to the investors and banks. But if the debt can be restructured and its repayment postponed for 10 years, the value of equity corresponds to a call that is still "out of the money" but can provide a time premium: thanks to the volatility of *EV*, established by past performance, the *EV* is capable of increasing beyond the outstanding amount of debt over the 10 years.

Supposing a volatility of 40% of the *EV*, the value of equity is 373, in the sense that the probability of bankruptcy is reduced from 100% to 74%. If the payment date is postponed to 20 years instead of 10, the time premium goes up and gives 528.

S = EV	800	800	800
E = D	1,000	1,000	1,000
Discrete r	2%	2%	2%
Continuous r	1.98%	1.98%	1.98%
σ	40%	40%	40%
Evaluation date	01/04/2015	01/04/2015	01/04/2015
Maturity date	02/04/2015	01/04/2025	01/04/2035
t (years)	0.00	10.01	20.01
d1	-10.64	0.61	0.99
d2	-10.67	-0.65	-0.80
$\Phi(d_1)$	0.00	0.73	0.84
$\Phi(d_2)$	0.00	0.26	0.21
Probability of bankruptcy: $1 - \Phi(d_2)$	1.00	0.74	0.79
Call premium = E value	0	373	528
Economic value of debt	800	427	272

Table 1.4. *Valuation of equity and debt using real options*

Such an approach allows us to obtain the economic value of the debt, which is the difference between the company value and the value of equity. If the debt reaches maturity tomorrow, there is no equity value; therefore, the value of the debt is 800, which corresponds to the raised funds if all of the assets were sold. If the debt reaches maturity in 2025, the value of the debt is reduced to 427, and to 272 if it reaches maturity in 2035.

The principle of limited responsibility also allows shareholders to abandon a company to investors if the value of the company is less than the outstanding debt. In other words, shareholders have a put over the totality of company assets that is exercised when a company defaults. If it turns out that the debt is risk-free, its present value would be $B = D.e^{-rt}$. But since it is a risky debt, its economic value must be reduced by the expected discounted loss by taking the risk of bankruptcy into account. The expected discounted loss, which is absorbed by investors, corresponds to the premium of the put (P), which is granted by the investors to the shareholders. Thus:

$$B = D.e^{-rt} - P \qquad [1.72]$$

Thanks to the call-put parity, using the usual Black–Scholes notations:

$$P = C - S + Ee^{-r\tau}$$

$$P = S.\Phi(d_1) - Ee^{-r\tau}.\Phi(d_2) - S + Ee^{-r\tau}$$
$$= S.[\Phi(d_1) - 1] - E.e^{-r\tau}[\Phi(d_2) - 1]$$

$$P = -S.[\Phi(-d_1)] + Ee^{-r\tau}[\Phi(-d_2)] \qquad [1.73]$$

with S = EV and E = D:

$$P = D.e^{-r\tau}[\Phi(-d_2)] - EV.[\Phi(-d_1)] =$$
$$\Phi(-d_2)\left[D.e^{-r\tau} - \frac{\Phi(-d_1)}{\Phi(-d_2)}.EV\right] \qquad [1.74]$$

$$B = D.e^{-r\tau} - \Phi(-d_2)\left[D.e^{-r\tau} - \frac{\Phi(-d_1)}{\Phi(-d_2)}.EV\right] \qquad [1.75]$$

$\frac{\Phi(-d_1)}{\Phi(-d_2)}.EV$ is the amount of debt which will be recovered by the investors if the put is exercised. Then, $\frac{\Phi(-d_1)}{\Phi(-d_2)}$ is the recovery rate and $D.e^{-r\tau} - \frac{\Phi(-d_1)}{\Phi(-d_2)}.EV$ is the expected discounted loss that will be absorbed by the investors given the hypothesis of the company default. Since $\Phi(-d_2)$ is the probability of bankruptcy, $\Phi(-d_2)\left[D.e^{-r\tau} - \frac{\Phi(-d_1)}{\Phi(-d_2)}.EV\right]$ is the expected discounted deficit. In the end:

Value of debt = Nominal value of debt – Probability of a default x expected discounted LGD [1.76]

where LGD[11] corresponds to the losses in case of a default.

11 Loss Given Default.

The time value of an option increases with the volatility of the underlying asset. Indeed, the more the company conducts its business in a market where the industry risk is great, the more the volatility of the economic assets will be high, impacting the rise in the value of equity. Because of this, real options provide a particular utility in valuating risky, expensive projects financed via debt (start-ups, mining and petrol industries, etc.).

1.4.2. *The impact of the risk debt on the time value of equity and the resolution of conflict between creditors and shareholders*

The time value depends on the position of the exercise price with respect to the price of the underlying asset. In other words:

– when a call is *out the money*, that is, the value of the economic asset is inferior to the amount of debt to be repaid, the value of equity is entirely made of time value. The investors then hope that the company's situation will improve, keeping in mind that the intrinsic value is zero;

– when a call is *at the money*, that is, the value of the economic asset is equal to the amount of debt to be repaid, the time value of capital can no longer grow. Since all scenarios are possible, the theory of real options finds its utility since it allows us to quantify the hope of investors;

– when a call is *in the money*, that is, the value of the economic asset is superior to the amount of debt to be repaid, the intrinsic value of equity quickly appears greater than the time value. The debt is less and less risky, and theoretically, it is without risk if the value of the economic asset tends towards infinity. The explanation depends on the fact that, when the value of the economic asset rises, the risk of probably bankruptcy falls, as well as the cost of the debt, which approaches the risk-free rate.

Finally, the time value rises with the maturity. A company in difficulty therefore benefits from an advantage if they renegotiate an increase in the maturity of its loans. Take for example a company with a debt of 50 payable in one year at an interest rate of 5%; we can conclude that at maturity, the company will have to pay its creditors 52.5 (50 x 1.05).

Supposing, moreover, that the economic value of the assets is 120, the value of capital that we can calculate using a classic approach is 70. By reasoning however using the logic of options, and taking the risk-free rate to be 3%, the present value of the debt including the payment of interest is 50.97 (52.5/1.03). The value of the debt can be considered as the difference between the value of the latter, discounted at the risk-free rate, and the value of a put.

In this case, the value of the put is 0.97 (50.97 – 50). The value of equity at 70 is split between an intrinsic value of 67.5 (120 – 52.5) and a time value of 2.5 (70 – 67.5).

Thus, in this example, we see that the time value (from the perspective of intrinsic value) and the premium of the put are limited. From that point, the interest rate of the debt is no longer considered to be 5%, but 10%:

– the amount the company must repay in one year to its creditors is 55 (50 x 1.1);

– the current amount of debt becomes 53.40 (55/1.03);

– the value of the deducted put is 3.4 (53.4 – 50);

– the value of equity at 70 is now split between an intrinsic value of 65 (120 – 55) and a time value of 5 (70 – 65).

As a result, since the probability of non-repayment of the debt increases, the premium of the put increases. Moreover, the equity risk is greater, which explains why its value incorporates more time value.

The appearance of hybrid financial products that combine equity and debts, such as convertible options or bonds with redeemable share warrants, is meant to fight against possible conflicts between shareholders and creditors. It is a way to give company creditors a call over equity. The conflicts between these different interested parties can be resolved as long as, if the shareholders have the power to make investment and financing decisions that can ruin the creditors, the latter have the option to exercise their share warrants or convert their investment into shares.

Jensen and Meckling (1976)[12] were determined to prove that the production of convertible investments reduced the risk to company asset substitutions with riskier assets by increasing the volatility of assets and, because of this, the value of equity.

In practice, when a debt arrives at maturity, a company repays a part of the amount using its available cash flow and refinances the remainder with a new loan. And even if, in theory, the cash flows are greater than the amount of debt to repay, they are generally generated over a longer lapse of time. In other words, the duration of cash flow is greater than the flows tied to the repayment of loans.

Consequently, the cash flows become insufficient from a liquidity perspective. The company is thus presented with the risk of rising interest rates and the risk of liquidity. The risk of liquidity cannot be covered because its cost can be considered excessive or, more simply, because the company can expect that it will never actually be exposed to such a situation. It therefore seems useless to prepare for it. Aït-Mokhtar (2008)[13] suggests that the difference between the duration of available cash flows and the duration of debt maturities is similar to company liabilities, just like a swap for which it would pay a variable interest rate and benefit from a fixed interest rate. This is to consider that at the maturity of its debt, a company will only have the option to repay it if it finds lenders, keeping in mind that the available cash flows are considered inconsequential for repaying the loans in question *in fine*. Thus, a company accepts getting into further debt in the future at an unknown interest rate.

If, in a healthy financial situation, the value of this liability is negligible, in a time of cash flow crisis or in the scenario where the repayment maturities are very near, this gap in refinancing can take on an entirely different value. It can correspond to the degree of uncertainty with respect to the future interest rate or, in theory, the very ability to cover costs. In this context, the value of equity – initially equal to the economic value of assets from which we must subtract the value of net debt – must be retired from the value of this financing impasse.

---

12 Jensen, M.C. and Meckling, W.H. (1979). Rights and production functions: An application to labor-managed firms and codetermination. *Journal of Business*, 52(4), 469–506.

13 Ait-Mokhtar, Y. (2008). Comment les mécanismes de protection peuvent affecter significativement le cours d'une action. *La Lettre Vernimmen.net*, 63, 1–4.

Thus, if the worry over the ability of the company to find new financing grows, then the value of equity is negatively impacted. Otherwise, it is possible to imagine that if this situation continues, the company lenders may wish to complete forward sales (overdrawn) of company shares to cover the risk of depreciation in the value of their debt securities. Hence, an increase in the stock market after an increase in capital can be justified. Indeed, this phenomenon can be explained as the way companies have found to refinance their debt.

If the value of the share lessens because of a transfer of value to the creditors, the refinancing impasse disappears – such that it is worth more than the reduction of debt – therefore positively impacting the value of equity.

1.5. Conclusion

The traditional valuation methods allowing us to estimate, *in fine*, the economic value of equity have the common disadvantage of not including the economic value of net debt and not eliminating the volatility of assets. Obtaining the value of a company using the structure of liabilities via the real options approach seems to be a pertinent complementary method. Indeed, considering that the economic value of equity is similar to the value of a call and that the economic value of net debt is analogous to the value of a put, the analysis through real options depends on the Black–Scholes formula (1973), which, moreover, makes volatility a major parameter. The convergence of optional models in discrete time and in continuous time favors the integration of dividend payments, and the emergence of a probability of bankruptcy and a recovery rate in the valuation confers a veritable added value to this innovative and dynamic method.

Financial literature proposed thereafter allows us to underscore the impact and stakes, both theoretical and empirical, of considering a net debt over the value of a company, and therefore over the economic value of equity. Taking new parameters into account, such as the costs of information, the costs of bankruptcy or protection clauses shows, once more, the adaptability of the real options approach, which strives to refine the reasoning as much as possible, in hopes of tending towards a more exact value.

2

The New Allocation of Company Value Using the Optional Approach

2.1. Introduction

The review of financial literature dedicated to optional valuation of equity is first reserved for Black and Scholes (1973)[1]. Their article presents a company financed by shares and investors whose assets are only made up of ordinary shares coming from another company. The bonds are zero-coupons and have a maturity of 10 years.

Moreover, the company plans to sell all of the shares it owns at the end of these 10 years, pay back the bond holders if possible and repay the remaining money to shareholders in the form of dividends. Under such conditions, the shareholders have an option over the company's assets that are financed by the bond holders. At the end of the 10 years, the value of equity, $w(x,t)$, is the value of assets, x, reduced by the face value of bonds if the latter is positive or zero. Thus, the economic value of bonds is $x - w(x,t)$. If the company holds company assets rather than financial assets and if, at the end of the period of 10 years, it creates new shares to reimburse the bond holders (and repay the remaining money to the initial shareholders so they can part with their shares), the economic value of bonds remains $x - w(x,t)$, where x is the value of the company.

Black and Scholes underscore that a rise in the company debt, with a constant company value, augments the risk of default and thus reduces the

1 Black, F. and Scholes, M. (1973). The pricing of options and corporate liabilities. *The Journal of Political Economy*, 81(3), 637–654.

market value of bonds. This has repercussions that are negative for bond holders and positive for shareholders. Thus, the price of bonds falls and the value of shares rises. It is in this way that variations in the structure of company capital can affect the price of a share, as soon as they become certain and not when they actually take place.

Thereafter, Merton (1974)[2] endeavors to define the economic value of debt, which, according to Galaï and Masulis (1976)[3], necessarily impacts the economic value of equity via the adjustment of systematic risk that it requires. Merton's valuation model of company debt does not include any rise in the value of the company through the tax rate generated by the fiscal deductibility of financial charges. This principle is the foundation for Modigliani and Miller (1963)[4], who established that the company value of an indebted company is equal to that of a debt-free company that benefits from the taxation economy.

In this context, the maximization of company value may result from the maximization of the company value that can result in the maximization of the level of debt. But, as Brennan and Schwartz remind us (1978)[5], such a conclusion leads to an inconsistency between the theoretical use that directors have for maximizing the weight of the shareholding and the empirical observations that show that companies do not maximize their debt reduction. Such a contradiction is explained by Modigliani and Miller themselves, who keep in mind that profits put to the side remain a less expensive source of financing than the acquisition of a debt, and insist on the need to maintain flexibility.

Other justifications, with respect to the limits on how much debt a company can take on, can be explained by bankruptcy costs that weigh on the value of the company, as shown by Kraus and Litzenberger (1973)[6].

---

2 Merton, R.C. (1974). On the pricing of corporate debt: The risk structure of interest rates. *Journal of Finance*, 29(2), 449–470.

3 Galaï, D. and Masulis, R.W. (1976). The option pricing model and the risk factor on stock. *Journal of Financial Economics*, 3(1/2), 53–81.

4 Modigliani, F. and Miller, M.H. (1963). Taxes and the cost of capital: A correction. *American Economic Review*, 53(1), 433–443.

5 Brennan, J. and Schwartz, E.S. (1978). Corporate income taxes, valuation and the problem of optimal capital structure. *Journal of Business*, 51(1), 103–114.

6 Kraus, A. and Litzenberger, R.H. (1973). A state preference model of optimal financing leverage. *Journal of Finance*, 28(4), 911–922.

Indeed, according to the authors, the level of taxation and the existence of bankruptcy costs create imperfections within markets that impact the market value of companies depending on their level of debt. Smith and Warner (1979)[7] examine the contracts for debts established between bondholders and shareholders. They are written with the purpose of managing conflicts of interest. Researchers note that direct restrictions on investment and production policies are expensive and difficult to follow while restrictions on dividend and financing policy, established following covenants, push shareholders to follow an investment and production strategy that maximizes value. Chava and Roberts (2008)[8] notice that agency conflicts interact on the financial structure, in particular, because of the presence of growth opportunities. Otherwise, the effects of a state of bankruptcy and the consequences of the dividend policies modeled by Leland (1994)[9] and Galaï and Wiener (2013)[10] affect the economic value of the net debt. Meanwhile, the model by Bellalah (2000)[11] includes protection clauses and information costs.

He and Xiong (2012)[12] note that the rise in credit risk following refinancing operations alters the liquidity of the company. The agency conflicts that result, because the shareholders cover any possible losses, increase the likelihood of bankruptcy. Charitou and Trigeorgis (2004)[13] remark that the latter is intimately linked to volatility. By being required to submit to refinancing a debt in order to preserve their percentage of control,

---

7 Smith, C. and Warner, J. (1979). On financial contracting: Analysis of bonds covenants. *Journal of Financial Economics*, 7(2), 117–161.

8 Chava, S. and Roberts, M.R. (2008). How does financing impact investment? The role of debt covenants. *Journal of Finance*, 63(5), 2085–2121.

9 Leland, H.E. (1994). Corporate debt value, bond covenants, and optimal capital structure. *Journal of Finance*, 49(4), 1213–1252.

10 Galaï, D. and Wiener, Z. (2013). The impact of dividend policy on the valuation of equity, debt and credit risk. Research paper, The Hebrew University of Jerusalem, Israel.

11 Bellalah, M. (2000). La structure du capital et les options : l'impact du coût d'information, de l'impôt sur les sociétés et du risque de défaut. Working paper, Université Paris-Dauphine, France.

12 He, Z. and Xiong, W. (2012). Rollover risk and credit risk. *Journal of Finance*, 67(2), 391–430.

13 Charitou, A. and Trigeorgis, L. (2004). Explaining bankruptcy using option theory [Online]. Available at: https://papers.ssrn.com/sol3/papers.cfm?abstract_id=675704.

those who hold the capital, according to Geske and Johnson (1984)[14], see their profit share as corresponding to the discounted expected future company value, reduced by the value of the debt and bonds to repay.

2.2. Economic value of debt and systematic risk adjustment of equity

Merton (1971)[15] introduces Ito's Lemma and the stochastic process in the construction of dynamic models in continuous time for an uncertain situation. He reminds us that this type of model is based on functions with geometric Brownian motion and on Poisson point processes. From the perspective of valuating the structure of liabilities of a company, Merton (1974)[16], like Black and Scholes (1973), considers the value of equity to be a call premium on the company assets and the economic value of the net debt. From this, Galaï and Masulis (1976)[17] model the repercussions of the economic value of the net debt and equity on the value of the company. They note that the systematic risk of equity and therefore the profit rate demanded by shareholders are necessarily impacted. They are thus interested in a study of the different financial structures impacting, *in fine*, the value of the company.

2.2.1. *Optional valuation of debt and the issues associated with getting into debt*

According to Merton (1974), the fluctuations of the value of a company, over time, are seen as a stochastic process according to the following differential equation:

$$dV = (\alpha V - C).dt + \sigma.V.dz \qquad [2.1]$$

14 Geske, R. and Johnson, H. (1982). The valuation of corporate liabilities as compound options: A correction. *Journal of Financial and Quantitative Analysis*, 19(21), 231–232.

15 Merton, R.C. (1971). Optimum consumption and portfolio rules in a continuous-time model. *Journal of Economic Theory*, 3(4), 373–413.

16 Merton, R.C. (1974). On the pricing of corporate debt: The risk structure of interest rates. *Journal of Finance*, 29(2), 449–470.

17 Galaï, D. and Masulis, R.W. (1976). The option pricing model and the risk factor on stock. *Journal of Financial Economics*, 3(1/2), 53–81.

where:

– α is the instant expected profit rate of the company by unit of time. If C is positive, it represents the total revenue by unit of time paid by the company to its shareholders and bondholders (e.g. dividends, interest charges). If C is negative, it represents the money received by a company for new financing;

– σ^2 is the instantaneous variance of the return for the company by unit of time;

– dz follows a standard Wiener process.

Moreover, F is the economic value of the debt and D is the nominal value of the debt, that is, the amount that the company has promised to repay to its bondholders according to a precise schedule. In the case where the repayment of D is not made, the bondholders take over the company and shareholders receive nothing. If there is no coupon, the stochastic differential equation applied to D gives:

$$\frac{1}{2}\sigma^2 V^2 \frac{\partial^2 F}{\partial V^2} + r.V.\frac{\partial F}{\partial V} - r.F + \frac{\partial F}{\partial t} = 0 \qquad [2.2]$$

Let us call:

– $F(V,\tau)$ the economic value of the debt when the remaining time to maturity is τ. Thus, $F(V,0) = min\ (V,D)$;

– $f(V,\tau)$ the economic value of equity when the remaining time to maturity is τ. Thus, $f(V,0) = max(0;V\text{-}D)$ and: $f(V,\tau) = V.\Phi(d_1) - De^{-rt}.\Phi(d_2)$.

Since: $F = V - f$, we have:

$$F = V - [V.\Phi(d_1) - D.e^{-rt}.\Phi(d_2)]$$

$$F = V.[1 - \Phi(d_1)] + D.e^{-rt}.\Phi(d_2)$$

$$F = V.\Phi(-d_1) + D.e^{-rt}.\Phi(d_2)$$

$$F = D.e^{-rt}.\left[\Phi(d_2) + \frac{V}{D.e^{-rt}}\Phi(-d_1)\right] \qquad [2.3]$$

Let us consider:

$$d = \frac{D.e^{-rt}}{V} \text{ or } \frac{V}{D.e^{-rt}} = \frac{1}{D} \quad [2.4]$$

Thus:

$$F = D.e^{-rt}.\left[\Phi(d_2) + \frac{1}{d}\Phi(-d_1)\right] \quad [2.5]$$

This formula allows us to express the exercise price of the risky debt. In this context, we call the return at maturity *R*. Then:

$$F = D.e^{-Rt} \text{ or } \frac{F}{D} = e^{-Rt} \text{ and } R = -\frac{1}{t}.\ln\frac{F}{D} \quad [2.6]$$

Consequently:

$$R = -\frac{1}{t}\ln.\left\{e^{-rt}\left[\Phi(d_2) + \frac{1}{d}.\Phi(-d_1)\right]\right\} \quad [2.7]$$

$$R = -\frac{1}{t}\ln.e^{-rt} - \frac{1}{t}\ln\left[\Phi(d_2) + \frac{1}{d}.\Phi(-d_1)\right] \quad [2.8]$$

$$R = r - \frac{1}{t}\ln\left[\Phi(d_2) + \frac{1}{d}.\Phi(-d_1)\right] \quad [2.9]$$

In the end, the spread is equal to:

$$R - r = -\frac{1}{t}\ln\left[\Phi(d_2) + \frac{1}{d}.\Phi(-d_1)\right] \quad [2.10]$$

Thus, the consideration of an economic value of net debt (substituting the amount of accounting net debt) in the process of company valuation necessarily impacts the systematic risk of equity and the profitability that shareholders demand from the company.

2.2.2. Combination of CAPM and the options model: the systematic risk of equity and the rate of return required by shareholders

Galaï and Masulis (1976)[18] combine the capital asset pricing model (CAPM) with that of options in order to valuate company equity. The

18 Galaï, D. and Masulis, R.W. (1976). The option pricing model and the risk factor on stock. *Journal of Financial Economics*, 3(1/2), 53–81.

synthesis of these models leads to an adjustment of systematic equity risk and to a distinction between different situations impacting the financial structure of companies. The authors recall the CAPM formula:

$$\bar{r}_i = r_f + \beta_i(\overline{r_M} - r_f) \quad [2.11]$$

with:

– $\bar{r}_i$: instantaneous return expected for a company share *i*;

– $\overline{r_M}$: instantaneous return expected from the market;

– β_i: instantaneous volatility coefficient for the share with respect to the market, also called the systematic risk of the share;

– r_f: risk-free interest rate;

– $\overline{r_M}$: – r_f: market risk premium.

And:

$$\beta i = \frac{\operatorname{cov}(\tilde{r}_i, \tilde{r}_M)}{\sigma^2(\tilde{r}_M)} \quad [2.12]$$

Thus, the present value of the company *J* can be found using the following expression:

$$V_0^J = \frac{\left[\bar{V}_T^J - \frac{\gamma \operatorname{cov}(\tilde{V}_T^J, \tilde{V}_T^M)}{\sigma(\tilde{V}_T^M)}\right]}{1+R_f} \quad [2.13]$$

where:

– *T*: liquidation date of the company;

– $\bar{V}_0^J$: final expected value of the company;

– $\tilde{V}_T^J$: economic value of company shares at maturity;

– $\tilde{V}_T^M$: economic value at maturity of shares from companies that make up the market;

– R_f: instantaneous risk-free market rate;

– $\frac{cov(\tilde{V}_T^J, \tilde{V}_T^M)}{\sigma(\tilde{V}_T^M)}$: risk unit;

– γ: market value by risk unit, defined by: $\frac{(\bar{R}_M - R_F)}{\sigma(\tilde{R}_M)}$;

– $\bar{R}_M$: expected market return in discrete time.

By using the Black–Scholes (1973) formula consisting of the valuation of a European call, Galaï and Masulis use the partial derivatives equation for the call formula in order to demonstrate the existing relationships between the different parameters[19]:

$$1 \geq \frac{\partial S}{\partial V} \geq 0; \frac{\partial S}{\partial C} < 0; \frac{\partial S}{\partial r_f} > 0; \frac{\partial S}{\partial \sigma^2} > 0; \frac{\partial S}{\partial T} > 0 \qquad [2.14]$$

Additionally, Galaï and Masulis retain the following Merton relations (1974)[20]:

$$\frac{\partial D}{\partial V} = 1 - \frac{\partial S}{\partial V}; \frac{\partial D}{\partial C} = -\frac{\partial S}{\partial C}; \frac{\partial D}{\partial r_f} = -\frac{\partial S}{\partial r_f}; \frac{\partial D}{\partial \sigma^2} = -\frac{\partial S}{\partial \sigma^2}; \frac{\partial D}{\partial T} = -\frac{\partial S}{\partial T} \qquad [2.15]$$

with:

– S: economic value of equity;

– V: economic value of assets;

– σ^2: instantaneous variance of asset returns;

– C: nominal value of debt;

– D: economic value of debt;

– r_f: risk-free interest rate;

– T: probable lifetime of a company.

The value of the share is a growth function of the value of company assets, the risk-free interest rate, the variance of returns of company assets and the maturity. On the contrary, it is a decay function of the nominal value of the debt.

19 See Appendix 1.

20 Merton, R.C. (1974). On the pricing of corporate debt: The risk structure of interest rates. *Journal of Finance*, 29, 449–470.

Following a stochastic logic and the hypotheses of a market in equilibrium by Galaï and Masulis (1976), the return on equity can be defined by the following expression:

$$\Delta S = S_V \Delta V + \frac{1}{2} S_{VV} \sigma^2 V^2 \Delta t + S_t \Delta t \qquad [2.16]$$

with:

$$S_V \equiv \frac{\partial S}{\partial V};\ S_{VV} \equiv \frac{\partial^2 S}{\partial^2 V} \text{ and } S_t \equiv \frac{\partial S}{\partial t} \qquad [2.17]$$

By dividing ΔS by S, we get, when t tends towards 0:

$$\frac{\Delta S}{S} = \frac{S_V}{V} V \frac{\Delta V}{V} \text{ or } \widetilde{r_S} = \frac{S_V}{S} V \widetilde{r_V} \qquad [2.18]$$

Now, according to formula [2.12],

$$\beta_S = \frac{\text{cov}(\tilde{r}_S, \tilde{r}_M)}{\sigma^2(\tilde{r}_M)} = \frac{S_V}{S} V \frac{\text{cov}(\tilde{r}_V, \tilde{r}_M)}{\sigma^2(\tilde{r}_M)} \equiv \frac{S_V}{S} V \beta_V \qquad [2.19]$$

Keeping in mind that, according to the Black–Scholes model (1973), $S_V = N(d_1)$[21], Galaï and Masulis combine the CAPM with the options model:

$$\beta_S = N(d_1) \frac{V}{S} \beta_V \equiv \eta_S \beta_V \qquad [2.20]$$

By replacing S with the call formula from Black and Scholes, we have:

$$\eta_S = N(d_1) \frac{V}{S} = \frac{V(d_1)}{V(d_1) - Ce^{-rf.T} N(d_2)} = \frac{1}{1 - \frac{Ce^{-rf.T} N(d_2)}{V(d_1)}} \qquad [2.21]$$

Now, $0 \leq S = V(d_1) - Ce^{-rf.T} N(d_2)$, which implies that:

$$\frac{Ce^{-rf.T} N(d_2)}{V(d_1)} \leq 1 \text{ and } \eta_S \geq 1 \qquad [2.22]$$

The systematic risk of equity is greater than or equal to that of the company, for $\beta_V > 0$. If the latter is stable, then equation [2.20] indicates

21 Additionally, given that $Dv = 1 - SV = N(-d1)$, $\beta D = Dv\frac{V}{D}\beta V = N(-d1)\frac{V}{D}\beta V \equiv \eta_D \beta_V$.

that the systematic risk of equity is not. Thus, K, the vector for the parameters V, C, r_f, σ^2 and T:

$$\frac{\partial \beta_S}{\partial K} = \frac{\partial \eta_S}{\partial K} \beta_V + \frac{\partial \beta_V}{\partial K} \eta_S \qquad [2.23]$$

and:

$$\frac{\partial \beta_S}{\partial K} \eta_S = 0 \qquad [2.24]$$

$$\frac{\partial \beta_S}{\partial K} = \frac{\partial \eta_S}{\partial K} \beta_V \qquad [2.25]$$

The existing relationships between β_S or β_D and the parameters of the vector K are[22]:

$$\frac{\partial \beta_S}{\partial V} < 0; \ \frac{\partial \beta_S}{\partial D} > 0; \ \frac{\partial \beta_S}{\partial r_f} < 0; \ \frac{\partial \beta_S}{\partial \sigma^2} < 0; \ \frac{\partial \beta_S}{\partial T} < 0 \qquad [2.26]$$

$$\frac{\partial \beta_D}{\partial V} < 0; \ \frac{\partial \beta_D}{\partial C} > 0; \ \frac{\partial \beta_D}{\partial r_f} < 0; \ \frac{\partial \beta_D}{\partial \sigma^2} \begin{cases} \geq 0 \\ \leq 0 \end{cases}; \ \frac{\partial \beta_D}{\partial T} \begin{cases} \geq 0 \\ \leq 0 \end{cases} \qquad [2.27]$$

The systematic risk of equity for a company is a growth function of the nominal value of debt and a decay function of the value of company assets, the risk-free interest rate, the variance of return on company assets and the maturity.

Next, Galaï and Masulis (1976) continue their study on the profitability rate required by shareholders. The instantaneous return on company assets is equal to that of its debt and equity weighted with their relative importance in the company accounts. Thus:

$$\bar{r}_V = \frac{S}{V} \bar{r}_S + \frac{D}{V} \bar{r}_D \qquad [2.28]$$

$$\bar{r}_S = \bar{r}_V + [2. \bar{r}_V - \bar{r}_D] \frac{D}{S} \qquad [2.29]$$

22 See Appendix 2, Appendix 3 and Appendix 4.

By replacing $\bar{r}_S$ by [2.11], β_S by [2.20] and recalling that $\beta_V = \frac{(\bar{r}_V - r_f)}{(\bar{r}_M - r_f)}$, we get:

$$\bar{r}_S = r_f + N(d_1)[2.\bar{r}_V - r_f]\,\frac{V}{S} \qquad [2.30]$$

According to Rubinstein (1973)[23]:

– $\bar{r}_V$ represents the expected profitability rate of company assets;

– $[2.\bar{r}_V - \bar{r}_D]\frac{D}{S}$ represents the financial risk of an indebted company taken on by the shareholders.

The equation [2.30] can also be written as:

$$\bar{r}_S = \bar{r}_V + [2.\bar{r}_V - r_f]\,[2.\eta_S - 1] \qquad [2.31]$$

Now, $[2.\bar{r}_V - r_f]\,[2.\eta_S - 1]$ represents the return on investment for shareholders, which includes the financial risk. From this:

$$[2.\bar{r}_V - \bar{r}_D]\,\frac{D}{S} = [2.\bar{r}_V - r_f]\,[\eta_S - 1] = [2.\bar{r}_V - r_f]\frac{Ce^{-rf.T}N(d_2)}{S} \qquad [2.32]$$

This result underscores the elements that contribute to a higher profitability rate, required by shareholders because of the debt. By using equation [2.11] and the results obtained in [2.26] concerning β_s, we have:

$$\frac{\partial \bar{r}_S}{\partial V} < 0;\ \frac{\partial \bar{r}_S}{\partial C} > 0;\ \frac{\partial \bar{r}_S}{\partial r_f}\begin{cases}\geq 0\\ \leq 0\end{cases};\ \frac{\partial \bar{r}_S}{\partial \sigma^2} < 0;\ \frac{\partial \bar{r}_S}{\partial T} < 0 \qquad [2.33]$$

In this context, Galaï and Masulis (1976) determined that it would be interesting to focus on different financial situations impacting the structure of capital and consequently the value of the company.

23 Rubinstein, M.E. (1973). A mean variance synthesis of corporate financial theory. *Journal of Finance*, 28(1), 167–181.

2.2.3. *Situations that impact financial structure*

In order to analyze the potential transfers of wealth from one security to another, Galaï and Masulis (1976) consider two companies, A and B, and define and then annotate the following variables.

Variables	A	B
Market value of company assets	V_0^A	V_0^B
Market value of company assets at maturity	V_T^A	V_T^B
Market value of company shares	S_0^A	S_0^B
Market value of company debt	D_0^A	D_0^B
Systematic risk of company assets	β_V^A	β_V^B
Systematic risk of company shares	β_S^A	β_S^B
Variance of return on company assets	σ_A^2	σ_B^2
Return on company assets	r_V^A	r_V^B
Return on company shares	r_S^A	r_S^B
Nominal value of debt	C_A	C_B

Table 2.1. *Variables for companies A and B for Galaï and Masulis (1976) analysis*

In order to study the impact of acquisitions and divestments, Galaï and Masulis consider the following hypotheses:

$$C_A = C_B \quad [2.34]$$

$$\overline{V}_T^A = \overline{V}_T^B \quad [2.35]$$

$$\text{cov}\left(\widetilde{V}_t^A, \widetilde{V}_t^M\right) = \text{cov}\left(\widetilde{V}_t^B, \widetilde{V}_t^M\right), 0 \leq t \leq T \quad [2.57]$$

$$\sigma_A^2 > \sigma_B^2 \quad [2.36]$$

Following [2.13], [2.35] and [2.36], the authors affirm that $V_0^A = V_0^B$. The two companies have the same systematic risk but different variances. If $\sigma_A^2 > \sigma_B^2$, then $D_0^A < D_0^B$ and $S_0^A > S_0^B$. Indeed, the value of the option is a growth function of the variance of its underlying securities, all other things being equal. Now, equity can be assimilated to a call. It is therefore possible to directly apply the relation $\frac{\partial S_0}{\partial \sigma^2} > 0$.

Two companies in possession of the same nominal value of debts and the same company value but with different variances will have different financial structures. The market value of $\frac{D}{S}$ will be greater for the company with the weaker variance. In the example, $\frac{D_0^A}{S_0^A} < \frac{D_0^B}{S_0^B}$. If a company makes an acquisition or an investment that modifies the variance of return on its assets, then the economic value of the debt and equity will be impacted.

In order to study the impact of the variation of the size of a company, Galaï and Masulis consider the following hypothesis:

$$\tilde{V}_t^A = \alpha \, \tilde{V}_t^B, 0 \leq t \leq T \qquad [2.37]$$

which implies that:

$$\tilde{V}_T^A = \alpha \, \tilde{V}_T^B \; et (\tilde{V}_t^A, \tilde{V}_t^M) = \mathrm{cov} \, (\tilde{V}_t^B, \tilde{V}_t^M), 0 \leq t \leq T \qquad [2.38]$$

Following equation [2.13], we have:

$$V_0^A = \alpha \, V_0^B \qquad [2.39]$$

Hypothesis [2.37] also implies that company returns have a perfectly positive correlation, such that:

$$\sigma_A^2 = \sigma_B^2 \qquad [2.40]$$

$$\beta_V^A = \beta_V^B \qquad [2.41]$$

If we consider that:

$$C_A = \alpha \, C_B \qquad [2.42]$$

Then, according to equation [2.17], which corresponds to the Black–Scholes formula, we remark that $d_1^A = d_1^B$ and that $d_2^A = d_2^B$. Therefore:

$$S_0^A = \alpha V_0^B N(d_1^B) - \alpha C_B e^{-rf.T} N(d_2^B) = \alpha S_0^B \qquad [2.43]$$

If the market value of assets and the nominal value of debts of two companies are proportional, then the economic value of their equity and their debt will also be proportional. If the value of a company rises by $\frac{\Delta V}{V}$, the latter can produce debt until $\frac{\Delta C}{C} = \frac{\Delta V}{V}$. This amounts to increasing the debt and the equity in proportion to the increase in the size of the company. In the contrary case, the company faces the dissolution of its securities (debt or equity).

In order to study the impact of fusions, Galaï and Masulis consider the following hypothesis:

$$\tilde{V}_t^G = \tilde{V}_t^A + \tilde{V}_t^B,\ 0 \leq t \leq T \qquad [2.44]$$

Now, according to the previous case:

$$V_0^G = V_0^A + V_0^B \qquad [2.45]$$

$$\beta_V^G = \gamma\beta_V^A + (1-\gamma)\beta_V^B, \textit{therefore}\ \gamma = \frac{V_0^A}{V_0^G} \qquad [2.46]$$

$$C_G = C_A + C_B \qquad [2.47]$$

$$\rho\ (\tilde{r}_V^A, \tilde{r}_V^B) < 1, \text{ where } \rho \text{ is the coefficient of correlation} \qquad [2.48]$$

Moreover:

$$\sigma_A^2 = \sigma_B^2 \qquad [2.49]$$

$$\frac{V_0^A}{C_A} = \frac{V_0^B}{C_B} \qquad [2.50]$$

Hypotheses [2.48] and [2.49] imply that:

$$\sigma_G^2 < \sigma_A^2 = \sigma_B^2 \qquad [2.51]$$

Hypotheses [2.44], [2.47] and [2.50] lead to:

$$\frac{V_0^G}{C_G} = \frac{V_0^A}{C_A} = \frac{V_0^B}{C_B} \qquad [2.52]$$

The study of the first case, results [2.51] and [2.52] and equation [2.17], which corresponds to the Black–Scholes formula, gives us:

$$S_0^G < S_0^A + S_0^B \text{ and } D_0^G > D_0^A + D_0^B \qquad [2.53]$$

The market value of debt for company *G* is higher than the sum of the market values of *A* and *B*'s debts. On the other hand, the market value of *G*'s equity is lower than the sum of the market values of *A* and *B*'s equity. The position of shareholders will deteriorate if the merger of companies *A* and *B* leads to a drop in the variance of asset returns for the new company *G*. As for the situation of *G*'s creditors, it is improved since the risk of bankruptcy has gone down.

In order to study the impact of splits, Galaï and Masulis consider the following hypothesis:

$$\tilde{V}_t^G = \tilde{V}_t^A + \tilde{V}_t^B, \ 0 \leq t \leq T \qquad [2.54]$$

which implies that:

$$V_0^G = V_0^A + V_0^B \qquad [2.55]$$

Company *G* is made of two economically independent divisions, *A* and *B*. At $t = 0$, company *G* separates from division *B*, thus *G* is composed only of division *A*. Thus:

$$C_G = C_A \qquad [2.56]$$

After the split, the creditors of company *A* (creditors of company *G* after the split) see their situation deteriorate since the assets that were backing the debt have diminished. The company that does not protect itself when financial decisions are being made can worsen the situation for its creditors.

Consequently, agency conflicts between the different interested parties of the company are provoked by the financial structure itself, by the strategies that are attached to it, as well as by the presence of investment options that give the company value a potential surplus.

2.3. Integration of organizational problems between shareholders and debtors

Myers (1977)[24] backs the idea that the production of risky debt in a context of holding onto growth options reduces the market value of a

24 Myers, S.C. (1977). Determinants of corporate borrowing. *Journal of Financial Economics*, 5(2), 147–175.

company in the sense that, in this case, the costs associated with this sub-optimal strategy are absorbed by the new creditors. Chava and Roberts (2008)[25] empirically study the mechanisms that tie investment decisions to financing decisions. They conclude that agency conflicts have an effect on the failure to comply with financial covenants and on investment expenses. The Morellec–Nikolov–Schürhoff model (2008)[26], which aims to define a capital structure that includes agency conflict, arrives at the conclusion that control revenues lead directors to take on less debt to balance the financial structure, which therefore becomes less advantageous for shareholders.

In the case of Galaï and Wiener (2013)[27], they present a Merton-type model by including the effects of a bankruptcy situation and the impacts of dividend policy on the value of debt and equity. The protection clauses and information costs are thus present in the contracts unifying the company investors in order to preempt agency conflicts.

Bellalah (2000)[28] considers them to be entirely different parameters, including them in his company option valuation model. Finally, Leland (1994)[29] considers the effect of taxes and bankruptcy costs on the economic value of the asset. In this context, he examines the definition of an optimal debt ratio and a critical threshold level for bankruptcy. According to him, protection clauses give a lesser value to companies that sign them because, in particular, their level of optimal debt is weaker. Moreover, it gives them a less onerous interest rate.

---

25 Chava, S. and Roberts, M.R. (2008). How does financing impact investment? The role of debt covenants. *Journal of Finance*, 63(5), 2085–2121.

26 Morellec, E., Nikolov, B., Schürhoff, N. (2012). Corporate governance and capital structure dynamics. *Journal of Finance*, 67(3), 803–848.

27 Galaï, D. and Wiener, Z. (2013). The impact of dividend policy on the valuation of equity, debt and credit risk. Research paper, The Hebrew University of Jerusalem, Israel.

28 Bellalah, M. (2000). La structure du capital et les options : l'impact du coût d'information, de l'impôt sur les sociétés et du risque de défaut. Working paper, Université Paris-Dauphine, France.

29 Leland, H.E. (1994). Corporate debt value, bond covenants, and optimal capital structure. *Journal of Finance*, 49(4), 1213–1252.

2.3.1. *The interaction of financing decisions*

Myers (1977) shows that the production of loans is inversely proportional to the portion of company value that is attributable to real options. Thus, even in the presence of favorable fiscal measures that aim to incite company debt, the optimal strategy encourages them to find a compromise between these fiscal advantages and the costs of this optimal strategy which need to be absorbed in order to envisage any future investment. The Myers article is, in many ways, in the continuum of the one by Jensen and Meckling (1976)[30].

These authors are in fact interested in agency costs and the optimal structure of capital. Myers, for his part, considers a sub-optimal investment policy to be an agency cost for a company. And Jensen and Meckling, as well as Myers, identify and analyze the costs that are traditionally considered imperfections of the market[31]. In this context, Mello and Parsons (1992)[32] recall the Modigliani–Miller principle (1963)[33], namely that in the absence of agency costs tied to debt, the value of an indebted company is equal to that of the debt-free company plus the fiscal deductibility of interest charges.

Then, Mello and Parsons overlap with Myers' work (1977) by taking an interest in agency costs of company debt in the mining sector. They note that as the size of the debt increases, the agency costs grow such that in situations where the debt is large, they can surpass the value of fiscal advantages tied to the fiscal deductibility of interest charges. In this case, the value of the company in debt can turn out to be less than that of the one that is not, insofar as we have to subtract agency costs from the company value adjusted for the fiscal advantage of interest charges.

Chava and Roberts (2008)[34] performed an empirical study on more than 37,700 loan contracts collected from more than 6,700 companies between 1994 and 2005. Their objective is to study the mechanisms that tie

---

30 Jensen, M.C. and Meckling, W.H. (1976). Theory of the firm: Managerial behavior, agency costs and capital structure. *Journal of Financial Economics*, 3(4), 305–360.

31 Jensen and Meckling discuss negotiation, follow-up and reinforcement costs of contracts.

32 Mello, A.S. and Parsons, J.E. (1992). Measuring the agency costs of debt. *Journal of Finance*, 47(5), 1887–1904.

33 Modigliani, F. and Miller, M.H. (1963). Taxes and the cost of capital: A correction. *American Economic Review*, 53(1), 433–443.

34 Chava, S. and Roberts, M.R. (2008). How does financing impact investment? The role of debt covenants. *Journal of Finance*, 63(5), 2085–2121.

investment to financing, that is, the friction caused by different financing methods that influence the choice of investments. The authors study these agency problems, namely the impact when the covenants associated with a company's investment debt are not followed.

In this context, they concentrate on the violation of restrictive financial clauses imposed on companies by creditors, such as the conservation of certain ratios or certain values. These violations, which the authors call "technical faults," caused by the fact that companies do not honor their commitments to pay off borrowed capital or interests, encourage the breakdown of financial alliances. In principle, the creditors then use their control rights and threaten to accelerate the schedule for repaying the credit. And these commitments are in fact omnipresent in financial contracts.

For example, public debt can exist alongside private equity. It is in these terms that the potential for violation exists and, moreover, as Gopalakrishnan and Parkash affirm (1995)[35], the non-respect of covenants arises in situations that are completely devoid of anger or any financial distress and only rarely leads to payment defaults or an acceleration of the debt repayment plan.

Thus, according to Chava and Roberts, the potential impact of violations of the covenants is not limited to a small fraction of companies confronted with unique situations. The authors study the impact of the transfer of control rights over the company investment. The optional logic suggests that the shareholders keep their rights of control as long as the investment value remains over a certain alliance threshold. In the inverse case, the rights to control can be granted to creditors, who then influence the company's investment policies. They can then increase interest rate, shorten the deadline for repayment, which reduces the free cash flow of the company, or become involved in subsequent investment decisions.

Chava and Roberts' study also shows that the transfer of control rights following a violation of the covenants, on average, leads to a fall in a company's investment activities by approximately 1% per quarter, since creditors intervene in order to prevent investments judged to be inefficient and also to punish the people responsible for the bad policy.

---

35 Gopalakrishnan, V. and Parkash, M. (1995). Borrower and lender perceptions of accounting information in corporate lending agreements. *Accounting Horizons*, 9(1), 13–26.

However, the authors point out a heterogeneity at the very heart of this phenomenon. Divestment is in fact more notable in cases where information and agency problems are larger than in cases where the friction from asymmetrical access to information are less severe. The authors even show that in cases where information and agency problems are less severe, the decrease in investment expenses is almost non-existent. It can occur in situations where the current creditors are long term and believe their client to benefit from a good reputation and where the loan was made before a bank federation (rather than only one credit institution).

For example, in line with the conclusions of Diamond (1989)[36], the authors note that on average, after a covenant violation by a company without any long-term moneylenders, the reduction in investments is 1.7% with respect to the value of shares while the companies with long-term moneylenders, on the basis of the same calculation, observe a negligible reduction in investments of 0.2%. Likewise, by referring to the works of Bolton and Scharfstein (1996)[37] which suggest an attenuation in the moral vagaries of borrowers, in the case of a covenant violation, companies under contract with a sole moneylender see a greater decline in investments (2.3%) than those who benefit from a bank federation (0.3%).

Morellec, Nikolov and Schürhoff (2008)[38] build a dynamic model of the structure of capital in order to determine if agency conflicts can explain the financial decisions of companies. The model contains variables such as tax on individuals or the costs of refinancing. Their analysis shows that the private profits linked to control lead managers to create less debt so they can rebalance the capital structure, which is often sub-optimal for shareholders. By using data on financing choices and by making predictions for different levels of debt, the three researchers observe that on average, 1.02% of agency costs on the value of equity is sufficient to resolve the issue of debt and justifies the chronological series of debt ratios observed. They also observe that agency costs vary between companies and that governance

36 Diamond, D. (1989). Reputation acquisition in debt markets. *Journal of Political Economy*, 97(4), 828–862.

37 Bolton, P. and Scharfstein, D. (1996). Optimal debt structure and the number of creditors. *Journal of Political Economy*, 104(1), 1–25.

38 Morellec, E., Nikolov, B., Schürhoff, N. (2012). Corporate governance and capital structure dynamics. *Journal of Finance*, 67(3), 803–848.

mechanisms significantly affect the value of control and the financing decisions of companies.

Galaï and Wiener (2013)[39] underscore the fact that the recent financial crisis made apparent the harmful effect of policies of excessive dividends leading companies to have financial difficulties. As Black says (1996)[40], "the more we look at the image of the dividend, the more it looks like a puzzle whose pieces simply don't go together". Benartzi, Michaeli and Thaler (1997)[41] find a very weak relationship between the variations of dividend payments and the content of information on the future beneficiaries of the company. Indeed, the increases (decreases) in dividends are correlated with the increases (decreases) in year-end and previous year results but do not explain any expectations on future profits.

Galaï and Wiener thus try to define the qualitative and quantitative restrictions on the dividend payment policy by taking any conflicts with creditors into account. The distribution of dividends, from the perspective of creditors, is similar to a reduction in company value and, consequently, increases the value of the put, the latter corresponding to the credit risk value. In other words, the forecasts for dividend payments over the lifetime of a bond loan can explain, at least in part, the overvaluation of bonds and the underestimation of their premium.

This is why DeAngelo *et al.* (1992)[42] observe that companies smooth out the payment of their dividends and try to maintain a stable distribution ratio. Moreover, it turns out that empirical studies before Galaï and Wiener's article on the spread of credit risk show that the latter are bigger than those anticipated by the classic optional model. Jones, Mason and Rosenfeld (1985)[43] consider the spread using the Merton model and observe that it is

39 Galaï, D. and Wiener, Z. (2013). The impact of dividend policy on the valuation of equity, debt and credit risk. Research paper, The Hebrew University of Jerusalem, Israel.

40 Black, F. (1996). Dividend puzzle. *Journal of Portfolio Management*, Special Edition, 8–12.

41 Benartzi, S., Michaely, R., Thaler, R. (1997). Do changes in dividends signal the future or the past? *Journal of Finance*, 52(3), 1007–1034.

42 Deangelo, H., Deangelo, L., Skinner, D.J. (1992). Dividends and losses. *Journal of Finance*, 47(5), 1837–1863.

43 Jones, E.P., Mason, S.P., Rosenfeld, D. (1985). Contingent claims valuation of corporate liabilities: Theory and empirical test. In *Corporate Capital Structure in the United States*. Friedman, B.M. (ed.). University of Chicago Press, Chicago, IL.

less than the one observed in the data. Elton *et al.* (2001)[44] as well as Huang and Huang (2003)[45] attempt to explain this surplus of premiums with unobservable variables such as the effects of tax rates or liquidity.

The Galaï and Wiener model is based on the conflicts of interest that exist between shareholders and bondholders. By establishing a stable policy of dividend distribution, shareholders certainly get value (expected) from the bondholders, but this stability facilitates surveillance by the bondholders. Indeed, Kalay (1980[46], 1982[47]) emphasizes that the restrictive clauses imposed on shareholders by bondholders push them to withhold dividends they would be authorized to distribute. The latter remain well within the imposed constraints. Thus, the bondholders can feel more secure with this accounting policy using covenants, projections and acceptable levels of probability of default. If a profitable company does not pay dividends (and does not develop a program for buying back shares), the value of the debt improves because of the decrease in probability of bankruptcy. If a dividend distribution program is expected without being realized, there is a transfer of equity wealth to the holders of the debt. Thus, the dividends are also a way of getting value from shareholders. A well-known and stable dividend payment policy, however, reduces the cost of the debt because the risk of credit is itself stabilized, making it more predictable.

In this context, Galaï and Wiener propose the introduction of a dividend distribution policy in the Merton model. They suppose that dividends are paid at a fixed, continuous rate. In this way, the shareholders of an indebted company keep a call over the company's assets in addition to having the right to obtain dividends. The dividends that are paid out reduce the value of the company, V, at a rate of δ and thus the put of creditors (which reflects the risk of credit affected by the fluctuation in dividends). By writing the value of the put over company V as P^{EX}, with an exercise price of F, T maturity and a risk-free rate of r, we have:

---

44 Elton, E., Gruber, M., Agrawal, D., MANN, C. (2001). Explaining the rate spread on corporate bonds. *Journal of Finance*, 56(1), 247–277.

45 Huang, J. and Huang, M. (2003). How much of corporate-treasury yield spread is due to credit risk? A new calibration approach. Working Paper, Penn State University, PA.

46 Kalay, A. (1980). Signaling, information content, and the reluctance to cut dividends. *Journal of Financial and Quantitative Analysis*, 15(4), 855–873.

47 Kalay, A. (1982). Stockholder-bondholder conflict and dividend constraints. *Journal of Financial Economics*, 10(2), 211–233.

$$P^{EX} = -Ve^{-\delta T}\Phi\left(d_1^{EX}\right) + Fe^{-rT}\Phi\left(-d_2^{EX}\right) \quad [2.57]$$

with:

$$d_1^{EX} = \frac{\ln\left(\frac{Ve^{-\delta T}}{Fe^{-rT}}\right)+\frac{\sigma^2 T}{2}}{\sigma\sqrt{T}} \quad [2.58]$$

$$d_2^{EX} = d_1^{EX} - \sigma\sqrt{T} \quad [2.59]$$

We can note that:

$$\frac{\partial P^{EX}}{\partial \delta} \geq 0 \quad [2.60]$$

The value of the put rises when the dividend distribution rate rises. Let us write B^{EX}, the price of the bond when the dividend is paid. Thus:

$$B^{EX} = Fe^{-rT} - P^{EX} \quad [2.61]$$

$$B^{EX} = Fe^{-rT} - \left[Ve^{-\delta T}\Phi\left(d_1^{EX}\right) + Fe^{-rT}\Phi\left(-d_2^{EX}\right)\right] \quad [2.62]$$

$$B^{EX} = Fe^{-rT}\,\Phi\left(d_2^{EX}\right) + Ve^{-\delta T}\Phi\left(-d_1^{EX}\right) \quad [2.63]$$

Using Boness (1964)[48] and Galaï (1978)[49] as a starting point, the probability of default *PD* when the bond loan is repaid, considering the dividend policy, is:

$$PD = \Phi\left(-d_{2V}^{EX}\right) \quad [2.64]$$

with:

$$d_{2V}^{EX} = \frac{\ln\left(\frac{V}{F}\right)+\left(R-\delta+\frac{1}{2}\sigma^2\right)T}{\sigma\sqrt{T}} \quad [2.65]$$

48 Boness, J.A. (1964). Elements of a theory of stock-option value. *Journal of Political Economy*, 72(2), 163–175.

49 Galaï, D. (1978). On the Boness and Black–Scholes models for valuation of call options. *Journal of Financial and Quantitative Analysis*, 13(1), 15–23.

Campbell and Taksler (2003)[50] observe that between 1995 and 1999, the American stock and bond markets evolved differently. That is, the price of shares rose sharply while the performance of bonds was mediocre. In fact, if the return on company bonds has risen, those on Treasury bonds will too, provoking stagnation in the spread. The authors explore numerous explanations:

– insofar as the shareholders predict better profits, they anticipate, optimistically, more revenues while the bondholders see neither more nor less than the anticipated coupon;

– the companies which resort to bond loans do not correspond to those that dominate the stock indices;

– a rise in the liquidity premium on company bonds with respect to Treasury bonds lowers the value of bonds without affecting the value of shares;

– the returns on newly issued company bonds can vary because of the change in characteristics. For example, a rise in the value of issuing impacts the drop in the price of newly issued bonds and the rise in their return without impacting the older bonds;

– given the expectation of future profits, the volatility of assets impacts bonds because of a rise in the probability of bankruptcy. To this end, Campbell and Taksler note that the more the volatility rises, the more the cost of the debt grows.

To mitigate agency conflicts, protection clauses and information costs figure in the contracts involving financing decisions. These are therefore two parameters to take into account in the valuation of a company using real options.

2.3.2. *Accounting for information costs and protection clauses*

Bellalah (2000)[51] seeks to optimize the value of companies by using the theory of options, first according to a model that conforms to those by Black

50 Campbell, J. and Taksler, G. (2003). Equity volatility and corporate bond yields. *Journal of Finance*, 58(6), 2321–2349.

51 Bellalah, M. (2000). La structure du capital et les options : l'impact du coût d'information, de l'impôt sur les sociétés et du risque de défaut. Working paper, Université Paris-Dauphine, France.

and Scholes (1973) and Galaï and Masulis (1976), then in a context that accounts for the effects of information costs with reference to the structure of capital, as envisaged by Bellalah and Jacquillat (1995)[52] and Bellalah (1999)[53].

The protection clauses preserve the interests of creditors. The general clauses allow for agreements between the different interested parties tied to financing and control operations. They reduce the influence of shareholders and directors in matters of financing and investment policy in order to limit transfers of wealth. The classic clauses that obligate the borrowing company to provide an exhaustive report of its activity fall within the scope of agency theory. The objective is to minimize conflicts of interest between different types of creditors. When special clauses are written, the company must use the loaned amounts to make profitable investments.

Additionally, because of the existence of different types of debts, a hierarchy is established. The senior debt, of the highest importance, is generally subject to securities on the assets of the borrower. The junior debt, of lesser importance, is repaid after the senior debt and is situated between equities and classic loans. The subordination clauses accompanied by special clauses, on their part, preserve the interests of each creditor.

The relationships that unite the shareholders, quasi-private equities and bonds, define the content of the clauses. The theory of options thus allows us to analyze them and evaluate the structure of liabilities.

A company with a value V subscribes to a bond loan of a face value of E and maturity T. The nominal of the debt can either correspond to a first-order debt P or a second-order debt Q. At the maturity of the debt:

– if $V > E$, the bonds are repaid at the amount of E and the value of shares S is equal to the residual value of the company $V - E$;

– if $V < E$, the company goes bankrupt. The creditors are partially reimbursed and the shareholders get nothing.

52 Bellalah, M. and Jacquillat, B. (1995). Options valuation with information costs: Theory and tests. *Financial Review*, 30(3), 617–635.

53 Bellalah, M. (1999). Les biais des modèles d'options revisités. *Revue française de gestion*, 025–124, 94–100.

The value of the option therefore becomes all the more important as the value of the company at maturity rises. Furthermore, investment in risky projects raises the value of equity[54]. When the bondholders are informed of a company's intention to proceed with a bond loan and modify its risk, protection clauses are included in the subscription contract.

We thus discover the benefit of the reorganization clauses in that they allow bondholders to begin proceedings for legal redress when the company does not respond to its obligations such as, for example, the payment of capital or interests. And creditors can begin bankruptcy proceedings when the value of the company reaches a critical level. Moreover, subordination clauses favor the hierarchization of the repayment of debt. In this context, a junior bond is repaid after a senior bond. At maturity, the value of assets for a company that has issued first-order bonds *P* and second-order bonds *Q* is:

	V < P	P < V < P + Q	V > P + Q
Senior bond	V	P	P
Junior bond	0	V – P	Q
Equity	0	0	V – P – Q

Table 2.2. *Value of the company on the maturity date of the financial debt*

The restriction clauses, which concern limits on creditors imposed over the dividend payment policy and on the charging of interest, can also protect bondholders against new issuing. The point is to include a clause that prevents the company from issuing new bonds without the agreement of second-order bondholders. Any new issuance of junior debt is in fact advantageous for first-order bondholders but unfavorable for second-order creditors.

The evaluation models thus relate to equity, debt and clauses present in debt subscription contracts.

The Bellalah and Jacquillat model (1995)[55] takes two new parameters into account: information costs for the share and information costs for the underlying asset. Thus, a call on the funds belonging to a company is equal to:

54 Galaï and Masulis proved in their article that: $\frac{\partial S}{\partial \sigma^2} > 0$.

55 Bellalah, M. and Jacquillat, B. (1995). Options valuation with information costs: Theory and tests. *Financial Review*, 617–635.

$$S = Ve^{-(\lambda_S - \lambda_V)T}N(d_1) - Ee^{-(r+\lambda_S)T}N(d_2) \quad [2.66]$$

with:

$$d_1 = \frac{\ln\left(\frac{V}{E}\right) + \left(r + \lambda_V + \frac{\sigma^2}{2}\right)T}{\sigma\sqrt{T}} \quad [2.67]$$

$$d_2 = d_1 - \sigma\sqrt{T} \quad [2.68]$$

– E: nominal value of the debt;

– λ_V: information cost relative to the economic asset of the company;

– λ_S: information cost relative to the value of shares;

– T: lifetime of a company;

– S: present value of equity capital;

– r: risk-free interest rate;

– σ^2: instantaneous variance on variations in the market value of the company.

Bellalah and Jacquillat (1995) studied variations[56] of equity capital value with respect to the parameters V, E, r, σ^2, T, λ_V and λ_S. And because $D = V - S$, we get:

$$1 \geq \frac{\partial S}{\partial V} \geq 0\,;\ \frac{\partial S}{\partial E} < 0\,;\ \frac{\partial S}{\partial r} > 0\,;\ \frac{\partial S}{\partial \sigma^2} > 0\,;\ \frac{\partial S}{\partial T} > 0 \quad [2.69]$$

$$\frac{\partial S}{\partial \lambda_S} > 0\,;\ \frac{\partial S}{\partial \lambda_V} > 0 \quad [2.70]$$

The results concerning the variables V, E, r, σ^2 and T are identical to those obtained by Galaï and Masulis[57]. The value of equity is a growth function of the company value, interest rate, risk and probable lifetime of the company. It is a decay function, however, of the nominal value of debt. The last two inequalities show that the value of equity is a decay function of

56 See Appendix 5.

57 See Appendix 1.

information costs in the sense that the derivatives are negative. In other words, a rise in information costs lowers the value of equity. Thus:

$$\frac{\partial D}{\partial V} = 1 - \frac{\partial S}{\partial V}; \frac{\partial D}{\partial E} = -\frac{\partial S}{\partial E}; \frac{\partial D}{\partial r} = -\frac{\partial S}{\partial r}; \frac{\partial D}{\partial \sigma^2} = -\frac{\partial S}{\partial \sigma^2};$$

$$\frac{\partial B}{\partial T} = -\frac{\partial S}{\partial T}; \frac{\partial D}{\partial \lambda_S} = -\frac{\partial S}{\partial \lambda_S}; \frac{\partial S}{\partial \lambda_V} = -\frac{\partial S}{\partial \lambda_V} \quad [2.71]$$

Bellalah (2016)[58] refers more generally to the "shadow costs", which the models for budgeting investments must include. The latter are irrecuperable and are made up of two elements. Following the Merton model (1987)[59] on the balance of capital markets in the presence of incomplete information, we first find the information costs tied to the imperfect knowledge of the market. It his article, Merton indicates that the effect of incomplete information on the price of equilibrium means applying an additional discount rate. In this context, the equilibrium of the expected return *Rs* on the share *S* is the following:

$$Rs = (r + \lambda s) + \beta s[Rm - r - \lambda m] \quad [2.72]$$

where:

– *Rm*: expected rate of return on the market portfolio;

– *R*: risk-free rate;

– *βs*: beta of the share *s*;

– *λs*: "shadow cost" tied to share *s*;

– *λm*: mean weighted "shadow cost" of incomplete information of all the securities in the market portfolio.

Let us note that in the presence of entirely complete information, the model becomes that of Sharpe (1964)[60].

58 Bellalah, M. (2016). Issues in real options with shadow costs of incomplete information and short sales. *The Journal of Economic Asymmetries*, 13, 45–56.

59 Merton, R.C. (1987). A simple model of capital market equilibrium with incomplete information. *The Journal of Finance*, 42(3), 483–510.

60 Sharpe, W. (1964). Capital asset prices: A theory of market equilibrium under conditions of risk. *Journal of Finance*, 19(3), 425–442.

Next, Bellalah indicates that we must consider additional costs caused by the constraint of short sales. In this context, Wu *et al.* (1996)[61] extend the Merton model (1987) to account for the restrictions on sales and the heterogeneous expectations of investors, that is, by considering two types of "shadow costs": λk corresponds to the constraint of information, and γk corresponds to the constraint of short-term sales. They thus develop a generalized model for the equilibrium of financial assets:

$$\mathrm{Rk} = (\mathrm{r} + \lambda\mathrm{k} - \gamma\mathrm{k}) + \beta\mathrm{k}[\mathrm{Rm} - \mathrm{r} - \lambda\mathrm{m}] \qquad [2.73]$$

The Black–Cox model (1976)[62], which evaluates reorganization and subordination clauses, has the objective of measuring their effects on the value of the financial securities of a company. They imagine a company that has signed up to a zero-risk bond loan paying shareholders a dividend δV. The percentage of dividends to pay is thus δ. In this context, the value of the debt B is the following:

$$\frac{1}{2}\sigma^2 V^2 B_{VV} + (r - \delta) V B_V - rB + B_t = 0 \qquad [2.74]$$

where:

– B: value of the debt;

– V: value of the company;

– σ^2: instantaneous risk of company returns;

– T: lifetime of the company.

The partial derivatives equation must satisfy the value of company assets. The following two conditions must be considered in order to resolve the equation:

$$\mathrm{B(V,T) = min\,(V,E)} \qquad [2.75]$$

$$\mathrm{B}\left(\mathrm{Ce}^{-\gamma(\mathrm{T-t})}, \mathrm{t}\right) = \mathrm{Ce}^{-\gamma(\mathrm{T-t})} \qquad [2.76]$$

61 Wu, C., Li, Q., Wei, K.C.J. (1996). Incomplete-information capital market equilibrium with heterogeneous expectations and short sale restrictions. *Review of Quantitative Finance and Accounting*, 7(2), 119–136.

62 Black, F. and Cox, J. (1976). Valuing corporate securities: Some effects of bond indenture provisions. *Journal of Finance*, 31(2), 351–367.

The first condition shows the value of bonds at the maturity date. The term $Ce^{-\gamma(T-t)}$ is the present value of coupons to pay bondholders. It also corresponds to the critical value of the company, synonymous with the triggering of bankruptcy proceedings. Likewise, the value of equity S is calculated using the following equation:

$$\frac{1}{2}\sigma^2 V^2 S_{VV} + (r-\delta)VS_0 - rS + S_V + aV = 0 \qquad [2.77]$$

The two conditions to resolve the above equation are as follows:

$$S(V,T) = \max(V - P, 0) \qquad [2.78]$$

$$S(Ce^{-\gamma(T-t)},t) = 0 \qquad [2.79]$$

With P as the value of senior debt, the first condition corresponds to the value of equity at maturity. The second condition proves that the bankruptcy proceedings are triggered once the value of the security is canceled. The value of bonds with this kind of protection clause is thus:

$$\begin{aligned}B(V,t) = {} & Pe^{-r(T-t)}\left[N(z_1) - y^{2\theta-2}N(z_2)\right] + Ve^{-\delta(T-t)}[2.N(z_3) \\ & + y^{2\theta}N(z_4) \\ & + y^{\theta+\xi}e^{\delta(T-t)}N(z_5) + y^{\theta-\xi}e^{\delta(T-t)}N(z_6) - y^{\theta-\eta}N(z_7) - y^{\theta-\eta}N(z_8)]\end{aligned} \qquad [2.80]$$

with:

$$y = \frac{Ce^{-\gamma(T-t)}}{V} \qquad [2.81]$$

$$\theta = \frac{r-\delta-\gamma+\frac{1}{2}\sigma^2}{\sigma^2} \qquad [2.82]$$

$$\delta = \left(r - \delta - \gamma - \frac{1}{2}\sigma^2\right)^2 + 2\sigma^2(r-\gamma) \qquad [2.83]$$

$$\xi = \frac{\sqrt{\delta}}{\sigma^2} \qquad [2.84]$$

$$\eta = \frac{\sqrt{\delta - 2\sigma^2\delta}}{\sigma^2} \qquad [2.85]$$

$$z_1 = \frac{\left[\ln V - \ln P + \left(r - \delta - \frac{1}{2}\sigma^2\right)(T-t)\right]}{\sqrt{\sigma^2 (T-t)}} \qquad [2.86]$$

$$z_2 = \frac{\left[\ln V - \ln P + 2\ln y + \left(r - \delta - \frac{1}{2}\sigma^2\right)(T-t)\right]}{\sqrt{\sigma^2 (T-t)}} \qquad [2.87]$$

$$z_3 = \frac{\left[\ln P - \ln V - \left(r - \delta + \frac{1}{2}\sigma^2\right)(T-t)\right]}{\sqrt{\sigma^2 (T-t)}} \qquad [2.88]$$

$$z_4 = \frac{\left[\ln V - \ln P + 2\ln y + \left(r - \delta + \frac{1}{2}\sigma^2\right)(T-t)\right]}{\sqrt{\sigma^2 (T-t)}} \qquad [2.89]$$

$$z_5 = \frac{[\ln y + \xi\sigma^2 (T-t)]}{\sqrt{\sigma^2 (T-t)}} \qquad [2.90]$$

$$z_6 = \frac{[\ln y - \xi\sigma^2 (T-t)]}{\sqrt{\sigma^2 (T-t)}} \qquad [2.91]$$

According to Black and Cox (1976), by designating $B(V, t, P, \delta\ Pe^{-r(T-t)})$, the value given by equation [2.80] for a bond paying P euros and including a protection clause ($\delta Pe^{-r(T-t)}$), the value of a junior bond is:

$$J(V,t) = B(V,t,P+Q,\delta Pe^{-r(T-t)}) - B(V,t,P,\delta Pe^{-r(T-t)}) \text{ for } \delta < 1 \qquad [2.92]$$

$$J(V,t) = B\left(V,t,P+Q,\delta Pe^{-r(T-t)}\right) - Pe^{-r(T-t)} \text{ for } 1 \leq \delta \leq \frac{P+Q}{P} \qquad [2.93]$$

$$J(V,t) = QPe^{-r(T-t)} \text{ for } \delta \geq \frac{P+Q}{P} \qquad [2.94]$$

Black and Cox thus show that protection clauses significantly augment the value of the debt modifying the financial structure. These clauses impose a "floor" value onto bonds and equity. Thus, shareholders lose control of a company the moment the company value tends towards a specified threshold for reorganization. It is moreover in the interest of bondholders to trigger the bankruptcy proceedings when circumstances allow, without waiting for the loan maturity date. Nonetheless, the bankruptcy proceedings are prohibited the moment the value of the company rises, that is, when a maximization strategy for the value is initiated.

2.3.3. Bankruptcy costs, getting into permanent debt and optimizing the debt ratio

Brennan and Schwartz (1978)[63] concentrate on the optimal structure of capital by accounting for the interest rate and bankruptcy costs. They suppose that the company value of a debt-free company, *U*, follows the geometric Brownian motion below:

$$\frac{dU}{U} = \mu . dt + \sigma . dz \qquad [2.95]$$

where *dz* is a standard Wiener process. The value of the indebted company, *V*, is a function of the value of the debt-free company (the two companies having the same assets), and of the time to maturity of the debt, *t*. In other words:

$$V = V(U,t) \qquad [2.96]$$

Thus, the partial derivatives equation is:

$$\frac{1}{2}\sigma^2 U^2 \frac{\partial^2 V}{\partial U^2} + r.U.\frac{\partial V}{\partial U} - r.U + \frac{\partial V}{\partial t} = 0 \qquad [2.97]$$

At maturity *T* of the debt, we have:

$$V(U,T) = U \text{ for } U \geq D \qquad [2.98]$$

$$V(U,T) = U - C(U) \text{ for } U < D \qquad [2.99]$$

where *C*(*U*) corresponds to the bankruptcy costs if the company is at risk of entering these proceedings. Furthermore, by supposing that t^- and t^+ respectively indicate the moments before and after dividend payments *d*:

$$V(U,t^-) = V(U - d,t^+) + d \qquad [2.100]$$

If the payment of coupons, *iD*, is included and τ is the tax rate on companies:

$$V(U,t^-) = V(U,t^+) - i.(1-\tau).D + i.D \qquad [2.101]$$

63 Brennan, J. and Schwartz, E.S. (1978). Corporate income taxes, valuation and the problem of optimal capital structure. *Journal of Business*, 51(1), 103–114.

where $i.(1-\tau).D$ corresponds to the rise in capital required to restore the company value of the indebted company after the payment of coupons. After development and simplification with $i.D$, we have:

$$V(U,t^-) = V(U,t^+) + i.D.\tau \quad [2.102]$$

If the dividends and the coupon are paid the same day:

$$V(U,t^-) = V(U-d,t^+) + d + i.D.\tau \quad [2.103]$$

Finally, taking bankruptcy costs $C(U)$ into account:

$$V(U,t^-) = V(U-d,t^+) + d + i.D.\tau. \text{ for } U \geq D \quad [2.104]$$

$$V(U,t^-) = U - C(U) \text{ for } U < D \quad [2.105]$$

The latter two formulas correspond to the necessary conditions for resolving the partial derivatives equation mentioned previously. But such an equation does not have a determinable solution. This is why Brennan and Schwartz use numerical techniques to determine optimal debt.

The Leland model (1994)[64] integrates taxes and bankruptcy costs when managers maximize the economic value of their assets and seek the optimal debt ratio as well as the possible level for bankruptcy. It supposes that capital is made up of perpetual shares and bonds paying out a coupon notated as C. The author considers two bankruptcy explanations:

– when the company no longer faces its obligations with respect to the repayment of its debts. In other words, bankruptcy is decided endogenously (the debt is not protected by any clause);

– when the protection clauses are included in the issuing contracts and trigger bankruptcy for a critical value of the company. Bankruptcy is decided exogenously: the clauses impose a "floor" value on the debt and equity.

In a previous article, Leland (1985)[65] already considered an optional model in continuous time, like that of Black–Scholes, containing transaction

64 Leland, H.E. (1994). Corporate debt value, bond covenants, and optimal capital structure. *Journal of Finance*, 49(4), 1213–1252.

65 Leland, H.E. (1985). Option pricing and replication with transaction costs. *The Journal of Finance*, 40(5), 1283–1301.

costs in order to balance a portfolio using enough cash to cover the option values. The Leland model (1994) uses the endogenous stochastic volatility function, which depends on all of the structural variables. By calling the simple Brownian motion W and the volatility of assets σ, the value V of the company follows:

$$\frac{dV}{V} = \mu(V,t)dt + \sigma dW \qquad [2.106]$$

Leland resolves the equation with the partial derivatives of Brennan and Schwarts (1978) by supposing that the company has infinite debt. The explanation comes from the fact that companies perpetually renew their debts. Just as in the Merton article (1973), F is the economic value of the debt, V is the company value and C is the payment of the coupon, by unit of time when the company is solvent:

$$\frac{1}{2}\sigma^2 V^2 \frac{\partial^2 F}{\partial V^2} + r.V\frac{\partial F}{\partial V} - rF + \frac{\partial V}{\partial t} + C = 0 \qquad [2.107]$$

Therefore, if there is no interdependence with time:

$$\frac{1}{2}\sigma^2 V^2 \frac{\partial^2 F}{\partial V^2} + r.V\frac{\partial F}{\partial V} - r.F + C = 0 \qquad [2.108]$$

Since the derivative only concerns V, the equation with partial derivatives can be simplified:

$$\frac{1}{2}\sigma^2 V^2 F''(V) + r.V.F'(V) - r.F(V) + C = 0 \qquad [2.109]$$

The solution to this partial derivatives equation requires the consideration of two scenarios:

– Exclusion of C. Thus:

$$\frac{1}{2}\sigma^2 V^2 F''(V) + r.V.F'(V) - r.F(V) = 0 \qquad [2.110]$$

This refers to the partial derivatives equation by Dixit and Pindyck (1994)[66], namely:

66 Dixit, A. and Pindyck, R. (1994). *Investment Under Uncertainty*. Princeton University Press, Princeton, NJ.

$$\frac{1}{2}\sigma^2 V^2 F''(V) + (r - \delta).V.F'(V) - r.F(V) = 0 \qquad [2.111]$$

with $\delta = 0$. In this case, the solutions of the characteristic equations are β_1 and β_2:

$$\beta_1 = \frac{-\left(r-\frac{1}{2}\sigma^2\right)+\sqrt{\left(r-\frac{1}{2}\sigma^2\right)+2.r.\sigma^2}}{\sigma^2} \qquad [2.112]$$

$$\beta_1 = \frac{-\left(r-\frac{1}{2}\sigma^2\right)+\sqrt{r^2-r\sigma^2+\frac{\sigma^4}{4}+2.r.\sigma^2}}{\sigma^2} \qquad [2.113]$$

$$\beta_1 = \frac{-\left(r-\frac{1}{2}\sigma^2\right)+\sqrt{\left(r+\frac{\sigma^2}{2}\right)^2}}{\sigma^2} \qquad [2.114]$$

$$\beta_1 = \frac{-\left(r-\frac{1}{2}\sigma^2\right)+r+\frac{\sigma^2}{2}}{\sigma^2} = 1 \qquad [2.115]$$

and:

$$\beta_2 = \frac{-\left(r-\frac{1}{2}\sigma^2\right)-\sqrt{\left(r-\frac{1}{2}\sigma^2\right)+2.r.\sigma^2}}{\sigma^2} \qquad [2.116]$$

$$\beta_2 = \frac{-\left(r-\frac{1}{2}\sigma^2\right)-\sqrt{r^2-r\sigma^2+\frac{\sigma^4}{4}+2.r.\sigma^2}}{\sigma^2} = \frac{-2r}{\sigma^2} \qquad [2.117]$$

The solution to the equation is consequently:

$$F(V) = A_1 V^1 + A_2.V^{-X} \text{ where } X = \frac{-2r}{\sigma^2} \qquad [2.118]$$

– Inclusion of C. The general solution to the partial derivatives equation is thus:

$$F(V) = A_0 + A_{1.}V^1 + A_2.V^{-X} \qquad [2.119]$$

The constants (i.e. A_0, A_1 and A_2) are determined by the bond conditions. Let us say that α is the fraction of value that would be lost due to bankruptcy costs, leaving the debtors with the value $(1-\alpha).V_B$ and the shareholders without anything at all, with V_B the level of company value at the moment when the bankruptcy is announced. Thus, the value of the debt, *D(V)*, is such that:

$$\text{If } V = V_B, \text{then } D(V) = (1-\alpha)V_B \qquad [2.120]$$

$$\text{If } V \to +\infty, \text{then } D(V) = \frac{C}{r} \qquad [2.121]$$

But if $V \to +\infty, V^{-X} = 0$, then condition [2.121] requires that:

$$A_0 = \frac{C}{r} \text{ and } A_1 = 0 \qquad [2.122]$$

Furthermore, taking condition [2.120] into account:

$$\frac{C}{r} + A_2 . V_B^{-X} = (1-\alpha)V_B \qquad [2.123]$$

Thus:

$$A_2 = \frac{(1-\alpha)V_B - \frac{C}{r}}{V_B^{-X}} \qquad [2.124]$$

and:

$$D(V) = \frac{C}{r} + \left[(1-\alpha)V_B - \frac{C}{r}\right] . \left[\frac{V}{V_B}\right]^{-X} \qquad [2.125]$$

where:

– C: debt coupon;

– *r*: risk-free interest rate;

– *α*: bankruptcy costs;

– *V*: asset value;

– V_b: asset value relative to the bankruptcy.

Considering the costs of bankruptcy *BC*:

$$\text{if } V = V_B, \text{thus } BC(V) = \alpha . V_B \qquad [2.126]$$

$$\text{if } V \to +\infty, \text{thus } BC(V) = 0 \qquad [2.127]$$

and if $V \rightarrow +\infty, V^{-X} = 0$, then condition [2.127] requires that:

$$A_0 = 0 \text{ and } A_1 = 0 \quad [2.128]$$

Moreover, taking condition [2.126] into account:

$$A_2 . V_B^{-X} = \alpha . V_B \quad [2.129]$$

Therefore:

$$A_2 = \alpha \frac{V_B}{V_B^{-X}} \quad [2.130]$$

and:

$$BC(V) = \alpha . V_B \left(\frac{V}{V_B}\right)^{-X} \quad [2.131]$$

Considering the tax rate on companies, *TB*:

$$\text{If } V = V_B, \text{ then } TB(V) = 0 \quad [2.132]$$

$$\text{If } V \rightarrow +\infty, \text{ then } TB(V) = \frac{\tau C}{r} \quad [2.133]$$

and if $V \rightarrow +\infty, V^{-X} = 0$, then condition [2.133] requires that:

$$A_0 = \frac{\tau C}{r} \text{ and } A_1 = 0 \quad [2.134]$$

Furthermore, taking condition [2.132] into account:

$$\frac{\tau C}{r} + A_2 . V_B^{-X} = 0 \quad [2.135]$$

Thus:

$$A_2 = \frac{\frac{\tau C}{r}}{V_B^{-X}} \quad [2.136]$$

and:

$$TB(V) = \frac{\tau C}{r} - \left[\frac{\tau C}{r}\right] . \left[\frac{V}{V_B}\right]^{-X} \quad [2.137]$$

Finally, taking bankruptcy costs and company tax rates τ into account, the company value *EV* is:

$$EV = V + TB(V) - BC(V) = V + \frac{\tau C}{r}\left[1 - \left(\frac{V}{V_B}\right)^{-X}\right] - \alpha . V_B\left(\frac{V}{V_B}\right)^{-X} \quad [2.138]$$

and the value of equity *E(V)* = *EV* – *D(V)*. Thus:

$$E(V) = V + \frac{\tau C}{r}\left[1 - \left(\frac{V}{V_B}\right)^{-X}\right] - \alpha . V_B\left(\frac{V}{V_B}\right)^{-X} - \frac{C}{r} - \left[(1-\alpha)V_B - \frac{C}{r}\right].\left[\frac{V}{V_B}\right]^{-X} \quad [2.139]$$

The absence of arbitration opportunities allows Leland (1994) to present the following formula for the evaluation of an indebted company's shares:

$$E(V) = v(V) - D(V) \quad [2.140]$$

$$E(V) = V - (1-\tau).\frac{C}{r} + \left[(1-\tau).\frac{C}{r} - V_B\right].\left[\frac{V}{V_B}\right]^{-X} \quad [2.141]$$

In addition, the expression for the company value proves that the value of the asset is maximized by the lowest possible V_B, which allows for the maximization of equity value, *E*(*V*), such that:

$$\frac{dE(V)}{dV} = 0 \text{ for } V = V_B \quad [2.142]$$

$$\frac{dE(V)}{dV} = 1 - X\left[(1-\tau).\frac{C}{r} - V_B\right].\left[\frac{V}{V_B}\right]^{-X-1}.\frac{1}{V_B} = 0 \quad [2.143]$$

For V = V_B:

$$V_B = 1 - \frac{2r}{\sigma^2}\left[(1-\tau).\frac{C}{r} - V_B\right].\frac{1}{V_B} = 0 \quad [2.144]$$

$$V_B = 1 - \frac{2r}{\sigma^2}\left[(1-\tau).\frac{C}{r} - V_B\right].\frac{1}{V_B} = 0 \leftrightarrow \frac{2r}{\sigma^2}\left[(1-\tau).\frac{C}{r.V_B} - 1\right] = 1 \leftrightarrow (1-\tau).\frac{C}{r.V_B} = 1 + \frac{\sigma^2}{2r} \quad [2.145]$$

$$V_B = \frac{(1-\tau).C}{r+\frac{\sigma^2}{2}} \quad [2.146]$$

Consequently, when bankruptcy is exogenous, V_B is proportional to C, independent of V and α. Moreover, if r, σ or τ rises, V_B decreases; finally, if C rises, V_B also decreases. Thus, by replacing the value of V_B obtained using [2.146] within [2.125], [2.139] and [2.141], we get:

$$\mathrm{D(V)} = \frac{\mathrm{C}}{\mathrm{r}}\left[1 - \left(\frac{\mathrm{C}}{\mathrm{V}}\right)^{\mathrm{x}} \mathrm{k}\right] \quad [2.147]$$

$$\mathrm{v(V)} = \mathrm{V} + \frac{\tau\mathrm{C}}{\mathrm{r}}\left[1 - \left(\frac{\mathrm{C}}{\mathrm{V}}\right)^{\mathrm{x}} \mathrm{h}\right] \quad [2.148]$$

$$\mathrm{E(V)} = \mathrm{V} - \frac{(1-\tau)\mathrm{C}}{\mathrm{r}}\left[1 - \left(\frac{\mathrm{C}}{\mathrm{V}}\right)^{\mathrm{x}} \mathrm{m}\right] \quad [2.149]$$

with:

$$\mathrm{k} = [1 + \mathrm{x} - (1-\alpha)(1-\tau)\mathrm{x}]\mathrm{m} \quad [2.150]$$

$$\mathrm{h} = \left[1 + \mathrm{x} + \alpha(1-\tau)\frac{\mathrm{x}}{\tau}\right] \mathrm{m} \quad [2.151]$$

$$\mathrm{m} = \left[\frac{(1-\tau)\mathrm{x}}{\mathrm{r}(1+\mathrm{x})}\right]^{-\mathrm{x}} / \, (1+\mathrm{x}) \quad [2.152]$$

Let us consider the coupon C that maximizes the company value V. By deriving equation [2.148] with respect to C, and by resolving the equation for C^* (optimal coupon), we have:

$$\mathrm{C}^*(\mathrm{V}) = \mathrm{V}[2.(1+\mathrm{X})\mathrm{h}]^{-\frac{1}{\mathrm{x}}} \quad [2.153]$$

By taking the value of C^* into account and replacing it within [2.147], [2.148] and [2.149]:

$$\mathrm{D}^*(\mathrm{V}) = \mathrm{V}\frac{[2.(1+\mathrm{x})\mathrm{h}]^{-\frac{1}{\mathrm{x}}}\{1-\mathrm{k}[2.(1+\mathrm{x})\mathrm{h}]^{-1}\}}{\mathrm{r}} \quad [2.154]$$

$$\mathrm{v}^*(\mathrm{V}) = \mathrm{V}\left\{1 + \frac{\tau}{\mathrm{r}}[2.(1+\mathrm{x})\mathrm{h}]^{-\frac{1}{\mathrm{x}}}\left[\frac{\mathrm{x}}{1+\mathrm{x}}\right]\right\} \quad [2.155]$$

$$\mathrm{V}_\mathrm{B}^*(\mathrm{V}) = \mathrm{V}\left(\frac{\mathrm{m}}{\mathrm{h}}\right)^{\frac{1}{\mathrm{x}}} \quad [2.156]$$

In the case where bankruptcy is determined exogenously, it is triggered thanks to protection clauses when the value of company assets is inferior to the value of the senior debt, notated as P. Let us consider that the senior debt corresponds to the market value of the debt when it is issued, notated as D_0. We thus consider here that $P = D_0 = V_B$. According to equation [2.125], the value of a protected debt at its issuance is:

$$D_0(V_0) = \frac{C}{r} + \left[(1-\alpha)D_0(V_0) - \frac{C}{r}\right]\left[\frac{V_0}{D_0(V_0)}\right]^{-X} \qquad [2.157]$$

When $\alpha = 0$, that is, when the bankruptcy costs are zero:

– the protected debt is less risky and pays the risk-free rate;

– the fiscal advantage coming from protected debt is inferior to that of unprotected debt;

– the value of assets related to bankruptcy for a protected debt is superior to the value of assets related to bankruptcy for unprotected debt.

Leland has shown that for $\alpha = 0$, the optimal level of bankruptcy V_B^* is the same for protected debt and unprotected debt. Additionally, for all $\alpha = 0$:

$$D_0^*(V_0) = V_B^*(V_0) = V_0\left(\frac{m}{h}\right)^{\frac{1}{X}} \qquad [2.158]$$

And if $\alpha = 0$, the debt is without risk, so:

$$C^*(V_0) = rD_0^*(V_0) = rV_B^*(V_0) = rV_0\left(\frac{m}{h}\right)^{\frac{1}{X}} \qquad [2.159]$$

$$v^*(V_0) = V_0 + \left[\frac{\tau C^*(V_0)}{r}\right]\left\{1 - \left[\frac{C^*(V_0)}{V_0}\right]^{X} h\right\} \qquad [2.160]$$

The conclusions of optimal financial structure analyzed by Leland (1994) are as follows:

– the maximum value of a company when there are protection clauses is usually inferior to that of a company whose debt is not protected;

– the value of a company when there are protection clauses is maximized if the tax on the company rises, the interest rates rise and bankruptcy costs fall;

– the optimal debt for protected debt is always inferior to that of unprotected debt;

– the interest rate paid for optimal debt is inferior for protected debt than for unprotected debt.

François and Morellec (2004)[67] analyze the impact of bankruptcy proceedings in American companies (via "Chapter 11 Bankruptcy") on their financing policy. The authors observe that the possibilities for renegotiating debt contracts prompt shareholders to default more easily, and to augment credit spreads. Because of this, these proceedings enhance the power of creditors to make decisions on financial policies for companies in difficulty. Moreover, the time constraints and the costs associated with this process of renegotiation affect the extent of these effects. In this context, it would be expedient to examine the impact of decisions to refinance debt on the value of equity.

2.4. Mechanisms of refinancing debt and the impact on the value of equity

By starting with the structural credit risk models by Leland (1994) and Leland and Toft (1996), He and Xiong (2012)[68] show that the deterioration of liquidity of the debt market brings about a rise in the liquidity premium on bonds, and of the credit risk tied to debt refinancing. When the deterioration of liquidity leads a company to undergo losses in refinancing its debts that are nearing maturity, the shareholders endure losses while the creditors are reimbursed in full. This type of conflict leads a company to have a higher probability of bankruptcy.

Contrary to Chen *et al.* (2007)[69] however, who consider the credit risk and the risk of liquidity to be independent variables, the He and Xiong model shows a complex interaction between the default premium and the

67 Francois, P. and Morellec, E. (2004). Capital structure and asset prices: Some effects of bankruptcy procedures. *Journal of Business*, 77(2), 387–411.

68 He, Z. and Xiong, W. (2012). Rollover risk and credit risk. *Journal of Finance*, 67(2), 391–430.

69 Chen, L., Lesmond, D., Wei, J. (2007). Corporate yield spreads and bond liquidity. *Journal of Finance*, 62(1), 119–149.

liquidity premium. As for Geske (1977)[70], he presents an optional valuation of liabilities model which suggests that repayment of debt is segmented into payment of coupons at intermediary dates before the total repayment of capital. Then, Geske (1979)[71], along the lines of Black and Scholes (1973) who define a share as an option on the value of the company, sees that a call on a share is an option on an option. After correction, Geske and Jonson (1984)[72] build on these works and continue with the scenario of a junior debt and a senior debt refinanced by equity. The operation then leads shareholders to integrally subscribe to a new issuance to preserve their percentage of control. The discounted value of their shares is, after refinancing, equal to the expected discounted future value of the company minus the nominal value of the junior debt and paid coupons. Finally, Charitou and Trigeorgis (2004)[73] present and test an optional model where the levels of volatility explain the state of bankruptcy, in particular.

2.4.1. *Risks of refinancing*

He and Xiong (2012) underscore the fact that assuming short-term debts aggravates the risk of refinancing. Acharya *et al.* (2011)[74], who are also interested in the risk of refinancing, show that a high frequency of use of short-term debt can lead to a diminished ability of the company to take on debt. Krishnamurthy (2010)[75] observes that the massive use of short-term debt such as negotiable creditor or repo securities was a key factor in the bankruptcy of Bear Stearns and Lehman Brothers.

70 Geske, R. (1977). The valuation of corporate liabilities. *Journal of Financial and Quantitative Analysis*, 12(4), 541–552.

71 Geske, R. (1979). The valuation of compound options. *Journal of Financial Economics*, 7(1), 63–81.

72 Geske, R. and Johnson, H. (1982). The valuation of corporate liabilities as compound options: a correction. *Journal of Financial and Quantitative Analysis*, 19(21), 231–232.

73 Charitou, A. and Trigeorgis, L. (2004). Explaining bankruptcy using option theory [Online]. Available at: https://papers.ssrn.com/sol3/papers.cfm?abstract_id=675704.

74 Acharya, V., Gale, D., Yorulmazer, T. (2011). Rollover risk and market freezes. *Journal of Finance*, 66(4), 1177–1209.

75 Krishnamurthy, A. (2010). How debt markets have malfunctioned in the crisis. *Journal of Economic Perspectives*, 24(1), 3–28.

In other words, the authors wish to use credit spread to show the dependency between the liquidity premium – tied to the illiquidity of the secondary market – and the default premium, determined by the credit risk. Empirically, this link, which the authors call the refinancing risk, is particularly visible when we observe the subprime financial crisis of 2007–2008 that led numerous companies to serious financial difficulties, which in turn amplified their credit risk.

The He–Xiong model adopts the exogenous framework of Black and Cox (1976) with regard to the notion of bankruptcy and determines the credit risk of a company by carrying out a joint evaluation of debt and equity. In this context, when a bond loan reaches maturity, the company proceeds to a new issuance with the same nominal value and the same maturity as the previous one. The market value (preserved) is either inferior or superior to the face value and the loss or the gain of refinancing is absorbed by the equity. Consequently, the price of the stock is determined by this future expected refinancing gain or loss and the net cash flow of the shareholders is:

$$NC_t = \delta V_t - (1 - \pi)C + d(V_t, m) - p \quad [2.161]$$

where:

– NC_t: value of shareholders' net cash flows after the issuance of a new bond loan (replacing the former);

– δ: dividend distribution rate (constant);

– V_t: company value;

– π: tax rate on companies;

– C: yearly coupon;

– $d(V_t, m)$: market value of the new bond loan with respect to the company value Vt and the maturity of the debt, m;

– p: nominal value of the bond loan to repay yearly.

The first term represents the dividends paid by the company. The second term represents the payment of a coupon after taxes. The third and fourth terms represent the gain or loss due to the refinancing of the debt. Thus, when $d(V_t, m)$ falls, the shareholders must cover the losses. Then, the value of equity reaches zero, the bondholders can recover their credit if the company assets are liquidated.

He and Xiong extend the scope of their research to include the structure of a bond market, similar to the one presented by Amihud and Mendelson (1986)[76], that is, bondholders are subjected to liquidity crises (with a Poisson occurrence ∝). During a liquidity crisis, the bondholder must sell their shares on the secondary market at a proportional cost k. In other words, the investor recovers a fraction $1-k$ of the market value of the bond. This transaction cost compounded by the intensity of the liquidity crisis determines the liquidity premium present in the credit spread of the company.

In this context, by deriving the evaluation of the bond, retaining V_B as the bankruptcy condition of the company, $d(V_t, \tau, V_B)$ as the value of a bond with a maturity of $\tau < m$, c as the annual coupon, p as the face value of the bond and r as the risk-free rate, the partial derivative equation is as follows:

$$\mathrm{rd}(V_t, \tau) = c - \propto . k(V_t, \tau) - \frac{\partial d(V_t,\tau)}{\partial \tau} + (r - \delta)\frac{\partial d(V_t,\tau)}{\partial V} + \frac{1}{2}\sigma^2 V_t^2 \frac{\partial^2 d(V_t,\tau)}{\partial V^2} \quad [2.162]$$

The left-hand side of the equation represents the necessary return the bond must generate. Within the right-hand side of the equation, the first term represents the payment of the coupon; the second term represents the loss caused by the occurrence of a liquidity crisis with the probability $\propto dt$ (when the event occurs, the bondholder is subjected to a transaction cost $k(V_t, \tau)$ when parting with the financial security at hand) and the last three terms capture the expected change in value due to a change in the maturity τ (third term) and a fluctuation in the value of the company V_t (fourth and fifth terms). We can write:

$$\mathrm{rd}(V_t, \tau) + \propto . k(V_t, \tau) = c - \frac{\partial d(V_t,\tau)}{\partial \tau} + (r - \delta)\frac{\partial d(V_t,\tau)}{\partial V} + \frac{1}{2}\sigma^2 V_t^2 \frac{\partial^2 d(V_t,\tau)}{\partial V^2} \quad [2.163]$$

The transaction cost causes the future value rate to rise markedly, which is the required return. Additionally, He and Xiong distinguish two conditions at the limits to define the price of bonds. At V_B, bondholders share the value of company liquidation proportionately. Thus, each bond gives:

$$d(V_B, \tau, V_B) = \frac{aV_B}{m} \text{ for } \tau \in [0; m] \quad [2.164]$$

76 Amihud, Y. and Mendelson, H. (1986). Asset pricing and the bid-ask spread. *Journal of Financial Economics*, 17(2), 223–249.

where a is a fraction of the company value resulting from the liquidation that the bondholders can recover.

When $\tau = 0$, the maturity of the bond is reached and its holder gets the capital p if the company does not go bankrupt:

$$d(V_t, \tau, V_B) = p \text{ with } V_t > V_B \qquad [2.165]$$

Consequently, by combining equation [2.162] with the conditions at the limits [2.164] and [2.165], the value of the bond is as follows:

$$d(V_t, \tau, V_B) = \frac{c}{r+\propto k} + e^{-(r+\propto k)\tau}\left[p - \frac{c}{r+\propto k}\right][1 - F(\tau)] + \left[\frac{aV_B}{m} - \frac{c}{r+\propto k}\right]G(\tau) \qquad [2.166]$$

where:

$$F(\tau) = N[h_1(\tau)] + \left(\frac{V_t}{V_B}\right)^{-2a} . N[h_2(\tau)] \qquad [2.167]$$

$$G(\tau) = \left(\frac{V_t}{V_B}\right)^{-a+\hat{z}} . N[q_1(\tau)] + \left(\frac{V_t}{V_B}\right)^{-a-\hat{z}} . N[q_2(\tau)] \qquad [2.168]$$

$$h_1(\tau) = \frac{(-v_t - a\sigma^2\tau)}{\sigma\sqrt{\tau}} \qquad [2.169]$$

$$h_2(\tau) = \frac{(-v_t + a\sigma^2\tau)}{\sigma\sqrt{\tau}} \qquad [2.170]$$

$$q_1(\tau) = \frac{(-v_t - \hat{z}\sigma^2\tau)}{\sigma\sqrt{\tau}} \qquad [2.171]$$

$$q_1(\tau) = \frac{(-v_t + \hat{z}\sigma^2\tau)}{\sigma\sqrt{\tau}} \qquad [2.172]$$

$$v_t = \ln\left(\frac{V_t}{V_B}\right) \qquad [2.173]$$

$$a \equiv \frac{r - \delta - \frac{\sigma^2}{2}}{\sigma^2} \qquad [2.174]$$

$$\hat{z} \equiv \frac{\left[a^2\sigma^4 + 2(r+\propto k)\sigma^2\right]^{1/2}}{\sigma^2} \qquad [2.175]$$

Keeping the price of the bond from equation [2.166] in mind, the return y from the bond is obtained by resolving the following equation:

$$d(V_t, m) = \frac{c}{y}(1 - e^{-ym}) + Pe^{-ym} \quad [2.176]$$

The right-hand side of the equation corresponds to the price of the bond, including the constant payment of a coupon over time and the nominal repayment at maturity, supposing that there is no default situation or other transaction in the meantime. Given that the price of the bond in equation [2.166] includes the transaction costs and the effects of bankruptcy costs, the credit spread (which corresponds to the difference between y and r) contains a liquidity premium and a default premium.

Furthermore, the value of equity $E(V_t)$ goes through the following differential equation:

$$r.E = (r - \delta)V_t E_V + \frac{1}{2}\sigma^2 V_t^2 E_{VV} + \delta V_t - (1 - \pi)C + d(V_t, m) - p \quad [2.177]$$

The left-hand side of the equation represents the necessary return on equity which must correspond to the sum of terms on the right side of the equation:

– the first two terms of the equation on the right capture the variation expected from the value of equity due to the fluctuation in the company value V_t;

– the third term corresponds to the cash flows generated by the firm in units of time;

– the fourth term corresponds to the detachment of the coupon after tax;

– the fifth and sixth terms concern the gain or loss of the refinancing after paying for the bonds close to maturity and creating a new bondholder loan.

He and Xiong affirm that, even in the absence of any constraint on the capacity to proceed with increases in capital, the deterioration of market liquidity of the debt can lead to a higher level of bankruptcy because of the increase in losses. The shareholders are thus ready to embrace the losses and pay back the creditors inasmuch as the value of the equity is positive. The value of an option to maintain company business thus justifies the absorption of costs tied to refinancing losses. In this case, the liquidity premium of company bonds, the probability of bankruptcy and the default premium increase.

The maturity of the debt plays a major role in the determination of refinancing risk. A short maturity reduces the bondholder's risk while it increases the company's risk of refinancing by obliging shareholders to quickly cover the losses from refinancing debt. The deterioration of market liquidity can have a significant effect on the credit risk depending on a company's rating and the maturity of its debt. For example, if an unexpected crisis brings about an increase of 100 basis points in the liquidity premium, the default premium of a company B with a debt maturity of one year increases by 70 basis points, which contributes to an increase in the total credit spread of 41%. Additionally, the same type of liquidity crisis increasing the default premium causes:

– for a company BB, with a debt maturity of six years, an increase in credit spread of 22.4%;

– for a company A, with a debt maturity of one year, an increase in credit spread of 18.8%;

– for a company A, with a debt maturity of six years, an increase in credit spread of 11.3%.

It would be useful to refine the study by trying to analyze the impact on the value of equity from the repayment of a debt with intermediate due dates.

2.4.2. *Reimbursing loans at intermediate intervals and the impact on the value of equity*

Geske (1977)[77] proposed a method for optional valuation of liabilities which includes $n - 1$ payments of individual coupons paid before the reimbursement of capital. Then, Geske (1979)[78] developed another model which refers to the one by Black and Scholes (1973). The latter considered that a share could be taken to be an option on the value of the company. From this perspective, a call on a share is an option on an option. Let us

77 Geske, R. (1977). The valuation of corporate liabilities. *Journal of Financial and Quantitative Analysis*, 12(4), 541–552.

78 Geske, R. (1979). The valuation of compound options. *Journal of Financial Economics*, 7(1), 63–81.

suppose V is the value of the company, S is the price of the share, D is the face value of the debt and K is the exercise price of the call on equity. Let us write t^* for the maturity date of the call on equity and T for the maturity date of the debt. The following figure illustrates Greske's principles, which lead us to consider the premium of an option.

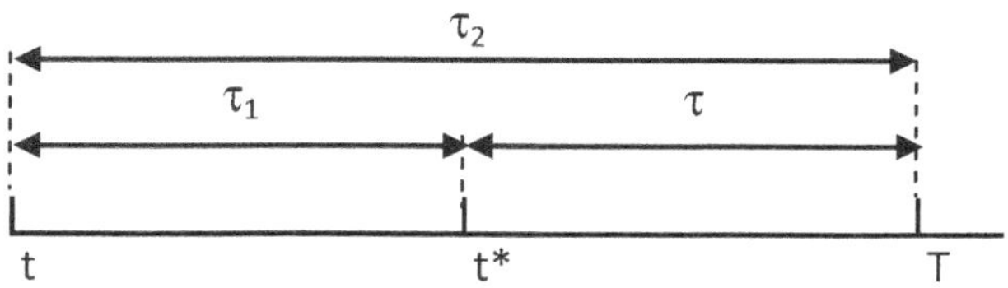

Figure 2.1. *Breakdown of a loan payment installment at an intermediary date*

On the intermediary date t^*, the holder of the call exerts their option on the share if the call is in the money, that is, if $S_{t^*} > K$. In the contrary case, if $S_{t^*} = K$ (or if $S_{t^*} < K$), then the call on the action will not be completed. Like the value of the share, S depends on the value of company assets, V, such a situation occurs when the value of the company V is equal to (or less than) V^*. Thus, V^* is the value of V such that $S_\tau - K = 0$. The holder of the call pays K at $t = t^*$ if, on this date, $V > V^*$ in order to maintain the possibility of paying D at $t = T$ to get company assets. In this case:

$$C = V.N(a_1, b_1, \rho) - D.e^{-r\tau_2}.N.(a_2, b_2, \rho) - K.e^{-r\tau_1}.\Phi(a_2) \quad [2.178]$$

where:

$$a_1 = \frac{\ln\left(\frac{V}{V^*}\right) + \left[r + \frac{\sigma_V^2}{2}\right]\tau_1}{\sigma_V\sqrt{\tau_1}} \quad [2.179]$$

$$a_2 = a_1 - \sigma_V\sqrt{\tau_1} \quad [2.180]$$

$$\rho = \sqrt{\frac{\tau_1}{\tau_2}} \quad [2.181]$$

$$b_1 = \frac{\ln\left(\frac{V}{D}\right) + (r + \sigma_V^2).\tau_2}{\sigma_V.\sqrt{\tau_2}} \quad [2.182]$$

$$b_2 = b_1 - \sigma_V\sqrt{\tau_2} \quad [2.183]$$

N(.) and *Φ(.)* are, respectively, the bivariate and univariate normal distribution functions.

By taking these principles as a starting point (all the while making a correction), Geske and Johnson (1984)[79] consider the case of a junior debt whose face value is M_2 with a maturity of T_1. In addition, Geske and Johnson suppose that $T_2 > T_1$ and that the senior debt is refinanced using equity. Thus, in order to maintain the percentage of control, on the date T_1, shareholders will all have to subscribe (at the level of their shares) to the new issuance. In this way, the present value of their shares after the refinancing of the senior debt will correspond to the expected discounted future company value, from which it is necessary to subtract M_2 (no possibility of bankruptcy is foreseen) as well as the future discounted payment on date T_1. This payment will only be made if no bankruptcy occurs in T_1, that is, if $S_{T_1} - M_1 > 0$ (where S_{T_1} is the value of equity at the moment T_1). Considering V^* the critical value of the company in case of bankruptcy on the date T_1 and J_{T_1} the value of the junior debt on the date T_1, and since $V_{T_1} = M_1 + J_{T_1}$, we get:

$$S = V.N(a_1', b_1', \rho') - M_2.e^{-rT_2}.N.(a_2', b_2', \rho') - M_1.e^{-rT_1}.\Phi(a_2') \quad [2.184]$$

where:

$$a_1' = \frac{\ln\left(\frac{V}{V^*}\right) + \left[r + \frac{\sigma_V^2}{2}\right]T_1}{\sigma_V\sqrt{T_1}} \quad [2.185]$$

$$a_2' = a_1 - \sigma_V\sqrt{T_1} \quad [2.186]$$

$$\rho' = \sqrt{\frac{\tau_1}{\tau_2}} \quad [2.187]$$

$$b_1 = \frac{\ln\left(\frac{V}{M}\right) + \left(r + \sigma_V^2\right).T_2}{\sigma_V.\sqrt{T_2}} \quad [2.188]$$

$$b_2 = b_1 - \sigma_V\sqrt{T_2} \quad [2.189]$$

79 Geske, R. and Johnson, H. (1984).The valuation of corporate liabilities as compound options: A correction. *Journal of Financial and Quantitative Analysis*, 19(21), 231–232.

The value of the senior debt B is the discounted value of M_1, given the full payment in T_1, to which we add the expected present value of the company value if the senior debt is not completely repaid. We then have:

$$B = M_1 . e^{-rT_1}\Phi(d_2) + V\Phi(-d_1) \quad [2.190]$$

where:

$$d_1 = \frac{\ln\left(\frac{V}{M_1}\right) + \left[r + \frac{\sigma_V^2}{2}\right]T_1}{\sigma_V\sqrt{T_1}} \quad [2.191]$$

$$d_2 = d_1 - \sigma_V\sqrt{T_1} \quad [2.192]$$

The correction by Geske and Johnson (1984) vis-à-vis the works by Geske (1977) comes down to the fact that the latter mistakenly gave the value of company assets each time $V < V^*$. But, when $M_1 < V < V^*$, the value of the senior debt should correspond to M_1 and the value of the junior debt should correspond to the remainder of the value. In this case, the value of equity is zero and the company goes bankrupt. Finally, the value of the junior debt J is the discounted value of M_2, given that no bankruptcy situation is expected, to which we must add the expected present company value if a bankruptcy situation occurs in T_2 and the payments arising in T_1 to repay the senior debt:

$$J = M_2 e^{-rT_2} . N(a_2', b_2', \rho') + V . N(a_1', -b_1', -\rho) + V\left[\Phi\left(-a_2' - \sigma\sqrt{T_1}\right) - \Phi(-d_1)\right] - M_1 e^{-rT_1} . \left[\Phi(d_2) - \Phi(a_2)\right] \quad [2.193]$$

with: S + B + J = V.

Charitou and Trigeorgis (2004)[80] try to analyze the default situations of 420 American companies between 1986 and 2001 by constructing a model inspired by the theory of options by Black and Scholes (1973), Merton (1974) and Vacisek (1984)[81] applied, in practice, by Moody's. Their results indicate that volatility plays a significant role in the explanation of bankruptcy situations, up to five years before they occur.

80 Charitou, A. and Trigeorgis, L. (2004). Explaining bankruptcy using option theory. [Online]. Available at: https://papers.ssrn.com/sol3/papers.cfm?abstract_id=675704.

81 Vasicek, O. (1984). *Credit Valuation*. KMV Corporation, San Francisco, CA.

Charitou and Trigeorgis thus consider equity to be perpetual call over the value of company assets. Nonetheless, contrary to the Merton model, which concentrates exclusively on payment defaults on the debt principal at its maturity, Charitou and Trigeorgis assume the non-payment by default of any planned installment, whether creditor interest or repayment of borrowed capital. In order to account for the probability of an intermediary default, the adjusted model lowers the conditions for default at maturity. The point is to resolve what is missing from the Vassalou–Xing (2004) model[82] which, if Vacisek's default limit is adopted, does not explicitly consider the probability of intermediary default often leading to negative expected growth rates (which seems incompatible with the theory of asset evaluation).

On the contrary, the Charitou–Trigeorgis model more closely resembles the one by Leland (2004)[83]. The latter analyzes different implications for limits on critical default and the relative performance of two default models: the first is being exogenous (corresponding to the Merton model) and the second turns out to be endogenous and refers to the works by Leland and Toft (1996)[84]. According to the latter, shareholders must decide if it is better to repay the debt or default on the payment. The Charitou–Trigeorgis model is analogous to the endogenous approach with the difference that they account for, at the start, the possibility of defaulting considering the cash flow hedge. It appears crucial for both researchers to consider the capacity of companies to face their obligations with cash and cash equivalents or flows coming from operating activities. Indeed, Leland does not include variables of liquidity. Additionally, he does not do an empirical study but rather creates simulations of data using Moody's notations which he compares with expected default probabilities (from simulations). Finally, the Leland model relies in large part on the financial structure of companies and the use of leverage, while Charitou and Trigeorgis include this intermediary default probability. In this context, Charitou and Trigeorgis distinguish two scenarios:

82 Vassalou, M. and Xing, Y. (2004). Default risk in equity returns. *Journal of Finance*, 59(2), 831–868.

83 Leland, H. (2004). Predictions of expected default probabilities in structural models of debt. *Journal of Investment Management*, 2(2), 5–20.

84 Leland, H. and Toft, K. (1996). Optimal capital structure, endogenous bankruptcy, and the term structure on credit spreads. *Journal of Finance*, 51(4), 987–1019.

– the probability of a voluntary default from shareholders (on interest and repayment of capital on the debt *I* at a moment *T'*):

$$\text{Prob}(\text{V}_{\text{T'}} < \text{V}^*) = \text{Prob}[\text{E}(\text{V}^*, \tau') < I] = 1 - \Phi(\text{d}_2^*) = \Phi(-\,\text{d}_2^*) \quad [2.194]$$

with:

$$\text{d}_2^* = \text{d}_2^*(\text{V}^*, \tau') = \frac{\ln\left(\frac{\text{V}}{\text{V}^*}\right) + \left[(\mu - \text{D}) - \frac{1}{2}\sigma^2\right]\tau'}{\sigma\sqrt{\tau'}} \quad [2.195]$$

where:

– μ: global return rate expected on the value of company assets (which replaces the risk-free rate);

– *D*: total distribution rate by the company to all its interested parties (including dividends and coupons) expressed as a percentage of the economic value of the company *V*;

– *V**: critical value of the company (lower than the value of the option);

– σ: volatility of company assets;

– τ': intermediary maturity remaining on *D*;

– *T'*: intermediary maturity of *D*;

– *E*: economic value of equity similar to a European call.

The higher the interest and repayment costs of debt *I*, the higher the probability of voluntary default at time *T'* will be. Additionally, the formula shows that shareholders can choose to default just before maturity if the value of the option is insufficient, that is, it is not enough to pay interest and the nominal amount. Liquidation is then very much voluntary. On the contrary, the default situation can be triggered by creditors if the company (profitable even from the point of view of the shareholders, i.e. $(V^*, \tau') > I$) does not have enough cash flow or liquid assets to repay the debt costs (interest and nominal). The default situation is then involuntary:

– the probability of involuntary default (on interest and repayment of the debt capital *I* because of a lack of liquidity at moment *T'*)

$$\text{Prob}(\text{cV}_{\text{T'}} < I - cash) = \text{Prob}[\text{CFC} < I] = \Phi(-\,\text{d}_2^*) \quad [2.196]$$

with:

$$d_2'' = \frac{-\ln\left(\frac{cV}{I-cash}\right)+\left[(\mu-D)-\frac{1}{2}\sigma^2\right]T'}{\sigma\sqrt{T'}} \qquad [2.197]$$

$$d_2'' = \frac{-\ln(CFC)+\left[(\mu-D)-\frac{1}{2}\sigma^2\right]T'}{\sigma\sqrt{T'}} \qquad [2.198]$$

where:

– *c:* proportion of cash from operating activities;

– *CFC*: cash flow hedge;

– Cash: cash and cash equivalents.

If the company generates a constant proportion of cash from operating activities, an involuntary default situation would be triggered at $T'(< T)$ if $c.V_T + cash < I$.

Charitou and Trigeorgis thus transpose the optional valuation model by Geske (1977) when the flows tied to repayment of a loan end up being paid at an intermediary date τ' when the maturity of the debt comes later. If at τ', V is smaller than V^* such that $E(V^*, \tau_1) - I = 0$, the shareholders will voluntarily default on the payment of the loan maturity. In this case, based on the notations by Geske, K is replaced by I and C is replaced by E (corresponding to the value of equity). The shareholders do indeed have the option to pay I on the intermediary date τ' to keep the possibility of paying M at $t = T$ in order to get company assets. In this case:

$$E = V.N(a_1, b_1, \rho) - D.e^{-r\tau_2}.N.(a_2, b_2, \rho) - I.e^{-r\tau_1}.\Phi(a_2) \qquad [2.199]$$

and the default risk at the intermediary date T is

$$P\,[2.E < I] = P\,[2.V < V^*] = \Phi(a_2),$$

where a_1, a_2, b_1, b_2 and ρ are the values defined by Geske (1979).

2.5. Conclusion

In the end, a company facing an unexpected increase in the variation of its returns due to a new investment project will see:

– the value of its bonds fall and the value of its shares rise;

– the systematic risk absorbed by shareholders rise and the one absorbed by creditors fall.

Jensen and Long (1972)[85] as well as Merton and Subrahmanyam (1974)[86] have demonstrated that a company, indebted or not, makes all its decisions with the objective of maximizing its company value. But the agency theory advocates for another strategy. Depending on whether shareholders control investment decisions, the company, given two investment opportunities with the same profitability but with different risks (the variance of returns of one of the projects being higher), will choose the riskier project.

In this context, we could even imagine a more profitable project being discarded in favor of another, riskier one. In this case, the company does not seek to simply maximize its value, but to optimize its financial structure. This theory can also be explained by the fact that the cost of capital, used by the company in its investment decisions, is a decay function of the variance of returns on company assets.

Finally, the deterioration of market liquidity of the debt accentuates the credit risk, for example, in the case of refinancing. Just like the level of volatility, the probability of bankruptcy increases because the losses are absorbed by shareholders and not by the creditors who must be repaid. The refinancing of a senior debt is thus done through the intermediary of equity.

At the end of the analysis of the literature on optional valuation of liabilities, we believed it worthwhile to conduct a recent empirical study with a large breadth of samples. It seeks to examine the performance of the real options method with respect to the traditional methods of valuation presented in the first chapter. The chosen approach conforms to the Black–Scholes–Merton model and applies to a multitude of business sectors[87].

It allows us to economically valuate the value of debt, that of equity and to identify the probability of bankruptcy of selected companies. The scientific articles of the literature review are not oriented towards the

85 Jensen, M. and Long, J. (1972). Corporate investment under uncertainty and Pareto optimality in the capital markets. *Bell Journal of Economics and Management Science*, 3(1), 151–174.

86 Merton, R.C and Subrahmanyam, M. (1974). The optimality of a competitive stock market. *Bell Journal of Economics and Management Science*, 5(1), 145–170.

87 The same as in the first chapter.

application of the real options method, strictly speaking, in order to valuate the structure of liabilities of a large sample of companies grouped by the business sector they belong to. They do not carry out comparisons with traditional valuation methods. The empirical financial literature presented in the second part is indeed dedicated to the study of the real options approach, particularly in a conjectural context tied, for example, to financial arrangements, bankruptcy situations or the impact of agency conflicts in company financing.

3

Applications of Real Options on Financial Structure Valuation

3.1. Introduction

The two studies presented in this chapter aim, first, to valuate samples of companies following the traditional methods[1] and following the real options approach. Next, statistical tests were performed in order to analyze the performance of the real options approach with respect to the methods used in practice by financial analysts. The objective is therefore to determine if the application of real options to the structure of liabilities can be a valuation method that complements traditional methods, that is, to know if the real options approach is dependable and pertinent. Real options in fact account for the economic value of the net debt and not its accounting sum, the average maturity of the debt, the volatility of assets and the probability of bankruptcy. In this context, it is possible that traditional valuations underestimate the growth potential of equity. Calculations at intervals of confidence and significance tests were thus made. The major differences between real options and the currently widespread approaches concern, in the case of real options, the inclusion of an economic net debt considering its maturity and the volatility of assets. The bankruptcy probability calculations and the rate of recovery complete the preliminary calculations.

The two studies can be distinguished by the nature of the sample. The idea was first to compare the approach of real options with the DCF method

1 The methods used are those of stock multiples (the calculations were made using forecasts from financial analysts on *zonebourse.com* and/or that of DCF (valuations directly made by brokers).

within the CAC 40 index. This application led to the conclusion that, with a risk of an error of 5%, the average differences of growth potentials of both approaches were equal. The explanation is due to the fact that companies in the CAC 40 are financially healthy (the probability of their bankruptcy is thus, on average, almost zero) and have a rather weak debt maturity. Thus, the value of equity from the Black–Scholes–Merton formula is not significantly different from the one obtained via the DCF method. Moreover, the equal differences of average debt ratios, based on the net economic debt, on the one hand, and on an accounting net debt, on the other, lead us to pronounce the pertinence and reliability of the real options approach.

Next, it seemed useful to orient the research not towards a stock index containing a homogeneous selection of companies in good health, but towards a rather heterogeneous business sector with respect to financial structure: the cinema industry. In this second application, the same approaches in terms of calculations and statistical tests were applied to 17 companies. And, in the same way, with an error risk of 5%, the differences in average growth potentials between the two valuation approaches were equal as well as the differences in averages between the two debt ratios (calculated using either a net economic debt or an accounting net debt). Consequently, the forecasts obtained via the DCF method of analysts are just as reliable as the Black–Scholes–Merton approach.

3.2. Application to the stock market index of a country: the CAC 40

Using data obtained on *Facset* and in reference documents from the sample companies, these empirical studies try to valuate companies from the CAC 40 using the real options approach and estimate the potential for growth of their stock price using this method and the DCF one. The statistical tests that follow attempt, in particular, to analyze the differences in significance between the growth potential of stock prices according to these two models, as well as between the debt ratios, based on the economic value of the net debt, on the one hand, and on its accounting value, on the other. The objective is then to judge the relevance and reliability of the approach via real options and perhaps identify a complementarity with the DCF method. The point is indeed to discern whether, when accounting for the economic net debt, the value of company equity is not underestimated. In the sense that the probabilities of bankruptcy and the average dates of maturity for company debt are reliable, the economic value of equity obtained using the DCF method and the real options is manifestly identical. Thus, it does not seem that the stock prices are underestimated.

3.2.1. *Databases, methodology and hypotheses*

Heller and Levyne (2014)[2] carried out statistical studies aiming to evaluate and test the growth potential of stock prices for companies in the CAC 40 index on February 22, 2013. On this date, four elements were taken from the Facset database for each company: the market capitalization, the volatility of shares corresponding to the standard deviation of daily returns over a time-scale of one year, the consensus of brokers over the value of the company and the target value of equity.

Insofar as many brokers use the DCF method to valuate, the insurance companies and banking institutions that make up the stock index were immediately put to one side. If Axa, Crédit Agricole, BNP Paribas and Société Générale can in fact be valuated using a cash flow approach, it nevertheless turns out that in this case, the latter correspond to a surplus of capital that could be transferred to shareholders by taking solvability constraints into account.

Thus, the cash flow can be considered a theoretical dividend that leads brokers to valuate these companies using an adequate method: the dividend discount model. Because of this, the sum of present values of expected free cash flows allows us to directly obtain the value of equity, the future value rate being the cost of capital. In the case of insurance companies such as Axa, the brokers use the target ratio of Solvency 1, in keeping with the target rating of the company. In the matter of banks, they take the equity ratio objective required by Bâle 3 into account. In other words, whether it is insurance companies or banks, no company value is included in the evaluation.

Furthermore, each daily volatility taken from Facset was multiplied by $\sqrt{252}$ in order to obtain yearly conversions. The risk-free rate taken was that of Treasury Bills at 10 years, namely 2.20% on the evaluation date, or 2.18%

2 Heller, D. and Levyne, O. (2014). Is the growth potential of stock prices underestimated? *International Journal of Business*, 19(4), 336–360.

in continuous time[3]. Additionally, the financial debts of each company in the sample were taken from their respective reference document at the close of business 2011.

Nevertheless, insofar as a company has a negative net debt, the use of the DCF method changes from one broker to another. Indeed, some calculate the present value of free cash flows by starting with the cost of capital, while others calculate the WAAC algebraically with a net negative debt. Voluntarily, given these possible divergences, the five companies with a negative net debt at the end of business 2011 – namely, Cap Gemeni, EADS, L'Oréal, STMicroelectronics and Technip – were removed from the studies. Moreover, Renault, whose weight in credit from client consumption is significant in their accounting, was also excluded from the sample. Consequently, the empirical studies focused on the 30 remaining companies of the CAC 40 stock index[4].

The growth potential of brokers was calculated by relating the target value of equity obtained by the DCF method to the daily market capitalization, then by subtracting 1.

By valuating the sample with the Black–Scholes–Merton approach, the bankruptcy risk of companies – by taking debt maturity and asset volatility into account – is integrated. Thus, the accounting debt, tied to the exercise price and removed from asset cash and cash equivalents to give a net debt, should not be overestimated since it relies on an economic value.

Because of this, the model should reveal the growth potential of the economic value of equity thanks to a new way of dividing the company. In the Black–Scholes–Merton articles, debt is indeed considered a zero-coupon. Consequently, the maturity date of the option corresponds to the residual maturity of the bond. Nevertheless, for numerous companies, the date is made of bonds generating coupons and financial loans from banks.

From a theoretical point of view, an option with different maturities should not be cast aside. However, in order to apply the Black–Scholes–Merton valuation mode, a residual average maturity τ for each of these company debts is assessed.

3 ln (1+ 2.20%).

4 See Appendix 6.

Table 3.1 provides the calculation details of the economic value of a debt using the Merton method and starting with the following hypotheses: a company value of 2,509, a risk-free rate of 2%, an asset volatility of 30% and an average maturity of 5 years for financial debts.

EV from DCF	2,509
D	1,00
σ from assets	30%
τ	5.00
r	2.00%
d1	1.86
d2	1.18
F(d1)	0.97
F(d2)	0.88
F(-d1)	0.03
Economic value of the debt	878
Economic value of equity	1,631

Table 3.1. *Economic valuation of equity debt using real options*

t	Volatility of assets					
	0%	10%	20%	30%	40%	50%
0	1,509	1,509	1,509	1,509	1,509	1,509
5	1,604	1,604	1,606	1,631	1,684	1,754
10	1,690	1,690	1,703	1,764	1,856	1,958
15	1,768	1,768	1,793	1,876	1,986	2,098
20	1,838	1,839	1,872	1,968	2,087	2, 199
25	1,902	1,903	1,942	2,046	2,165	2,272

Table 3.2. *Sensitivity of the economic value of equity*

Table 3.2 shows that the equity value from the DCF method (1,509) is only obtained if the maturity date, that is, the residual average maturity of the financial debt, is zero. Otherwise, the greater the maturity, the higher the time value and the value of equity rises. Moreover, the higher the volatility, the more the probability of a rise in stock prices also goes up, which implies a rise in the value of equity.

In order to apply the model to the data, the company values and their volatility had to be estimated. The volatility of underlying assets corresponds in fact to the volatility of the company value. But the assets are rarely priced, except for company holdings which are not represented in the CAC 40 stock index. Consequently, the estimate of the company value and its volatility are based on the methodology proposed by Hull *et al.* (2005)[5] and commonly used by Moody's notation agency. Using the Ito lemma as a basis:

$$dF(x,t) = \left[\frac{\partial F}{\partial t} + \alpha(x,t)\frac{\partial F}{\partial x} + \frac{1}{2}b^2(x,t)\frac{\partial^2 F}{\partial x^2}\right]dt + b(x,t)\frac{\partial F}{\partial x}dz \quad [3.1]$$

Thus, by replacing:

– F by E (for the value of equity);

– x by EV (for company value);

– $a(x,t) = m.EV$;

– and $b(x,t) = \sigma_{EV}.EV$ where σ_V corresponds to the volatility of assets or of the company value.

$$dE(EV,t) = \left[\frac{\partial E}{\partial t} + m.EV\frac{\partial E}{\partial EV} + \frac{1}{2}\sigma_{EV}^2 EV^2\frac{\partial^2 E}{\partial EV^2}\right]dt + \sigma_V EV\frac{\partial E}{\partial EV}dz \quad [3.2]$$

$$\sigma_{EV}EV\,\frac{\partial CP}{\partial VE}dz = \sigma_E E.\,dz \text{ and } \sigma_{EV}EV\,\frac{\partial CP}{\partial VE} = \sigma_E E \quad [3.3]$$

$$\sigma_E E = \sigma_{EV}EV\,.\,\Phi(d_1) \quad [3.4]$$

where σ_E corresponds to the volatility of shares.

Additionally, thanks to the Merton formula:

$$E = V.\,\Phi(d_1) - De^{-rt}.\Phi(d_2) + TA \quad [3.5]$$

5 Hull, J.C., Nelken, I., White, A. (2005). Merton's model, credit risk and volatility skews. *Journal of Credit Risk*, 1(1), 3–28.

The values of EV and σ_{EV} can be obtained using the Excel calculator applied to the following nonlinear system:

$$\mathrm{EV}.\Phi\left[\frac{\ln\left(\frac{\mathrm{EV}}{\mathrm{D}}\right)+\left(\mathrm{r}+\frac{\sigma_{\mathrm{EV}}^2}{2}\right).\tau}{\sigma_{\mathrm{EV}}\sqrt{\tau}}\right]-\mathrm{De}^{-\mathrm{r}\tau}.\Phi\left[\frac{\ln\left(\frac{\mathrm{EV}}{\mathrm{D}}\right)+\left(\mathrm{r}-\frac{\sigma_{\mathrm{EV}}^2}{2}\right)\tau}{\sigma_{\mathrm{EV}}\sqrt{\tau}}\right]=\mathrm{E} \qquad [3.6]$$

$$\frac{\sigma_{\mathrm{EV}}.\mathrm{EV}.\Phi\left[\frac{\ln\left(\frac{\mathrm{EV}}{\mathrm{D}}\right)+\left(\mathrm{r}+\frac{\sigma_{\mathrm{EV}}^2}{2}\right).\tau}{\sigma_{\mathrm{EV}}\sqrt{\tau}}\right]}{\mathrm{E}}=\sigma_{\mathrm{E}} \qquad [3.7]$$

To solve this system, the following parameters are considered:

– E = daily stock capitalization;

– D = net accounting debt taken from financial reports;

– τ= the average residual maturity of the debt calculated using the repayment calendar for the debt;

– σ_E = the volatility of shares taken from Facset and then annualized;

– r = the continuous risk-free rate of 2.18% corresponding to the OAT French rates at 10 years.

Once the company value and its volatility have been calculated (produced by the calculator), the Black–Scholes–Merton valuation model for each company was applied in order to find the economic value of equity and the net debt. In this case:

$$\mathrm{E}=\mathrm{EV}-[\mathrm{EV}.\Phi(-\mathrm{d}_1)+\mathrm{De}^{-\mathrm{r}\tau}.\Phi(\mathrm{d}_2)-\mathrm{TA}] \qquad [3.8]$$

with:

$$\mathrm{d}_1=\frac{\ln\left(\frac{\mathrm{EV}}{\mathrm{D}}\right)+\left(\mathrm{r}+\frac{\sigma_{\mathrm{EV}}^2}{2}\right)\tau}{\sigma_{\mathrm{EV}}\sqrt{\tau}} \text{ and } \mathrm{d}_2=\mathrm{d}_1-\sigma_{\mathrm{EV}}\sqrt{\tau} \qquad [3.9]$$

where:

– E: economic value of equity;

– EV: company value according to broker consensus (DCF);

– $\Phi(.)$: normal standard distribution;

– D: accounting debt;

– TA: cash and cash equivalents.

An alternative approach allows us to estimate the value of economic debt for Merton, called B:

$$B = EV.\Phi(-d_1) + De^{-r\tau}.\Phi(d_2) - De^{-r\tau} + De^{-r\tau} \quad [3.10]$$

$$B = De^{-r\tau} + EV.\Phi(-d_1) + De^{-r\tau}.[\Phi(d_2) - 1] \quad [3.11]$$

$$B = De^{-r\tau} + EV.\Phi(-d_1) + De^{-r\tau}.\Phi(-d_2) \quad [3.12]$$

$$B = De^{-r\tau} - \Phi(-d_2)\left[De^{-r\tau} - \frac{\Phi(-d_1)}{\Phi(-d_2)}EV\right] \quad [3.13]$$

$\frac{\Phi(-d_1)}{\Phi(-d_2)}EV$ is the amount of debt that will be recovered bondholders if the company goes bankrupt.

Then, $\frac{\Phi(-d_1)}{\Phi(-d_2)}$ is the recovery rate and $De^{-r\tau} - \frac{\Phi(-d_1)}{\Phi(-d_2)}EV$ the expected discounted loss, written LGD[6], which would be absorbed by bondholders in the case of the supposed default by the company. Since $\Phi(-d_2)$ is the bankruptcy risk, $\Phi(-d_2)\left[De^{-r\tau} - \frac{\Phi(-d_1)}{\Phi(-d_2)}EV\right]$ is the expected discounted loss of earnings. Finally, as used by Moody's KMV and the risk management hubs at banks in determining the calculations for weighing asset risk:

$$B = De^{-r\tau} - \Phi(-d_2).\text{LGD} \quad [3.14]$$

The three principal parameters of the economic value of the net debt seem to be its maturity (τ), the recovery rate for the level of bankruptcy $\left(\frac{\Phi(-d_1)}{\Phi(-d_2)}\right)$, which includes the risk of bankruptcy, and the weight of its face value, which is expressed as a percentage of the company value (*D/EV*). In

6 Loss Given Default.

this case, a multiple regression is tested to justify the potential for growth based on the value of equity by Black–Scholes–Merton[7].

The empirical studies therefore concentrate on the potential for growth in stock prices for the 30 companies listed in the CAC 40, based on target values established by brokers, and on the values obtained using the real options approach. They are compared, systematically, to the market capitalization on the day of the evaluation[8]. In the first case, the target value is the company value, which corresponds to the present value of future free cash flows, determined by brokers, minus the net debt found in financial reports. In the second case, the Black–Scholes–Merton approach proposes a new way of dividing the value of a company obtained by the DCF method between equity values and economic debt.

The hypotheses, with respect to the results that will be obtained, are as follows:

– the differences in significance between the volatility of shares (σE) and that of assets (σV) should be equal, allowing us to justify taking the volatility of assets into account (instead of shares) in the method of valuation using real options;

– the differences in significance between the percentage of evolution of stock prices for the companies in the sample using the DCF method and the real options method should be equal, allowing us to justify the relevance of using the real options method;

– the differences in equal significance between two growth potentials can be explained by the respective debt ratios. This is the reason why it seemed useful to test the ratio of net debt on the company value, calculated on the basis of the accounting net debt, on the one hand, and referring to the economic value (obtained by the Black–Scholes–Merton method), on the other. These ratios are written *D/EV* and *B/EV*, respectively. The differences in significance between these ratios should be equal, allowing us to justify using the economic debt.

7 See Appendix 7 and Appendix 8.

8 The growth potentials are obtained by carrying over the valuation of market capitalization from which we subtract 1.

3.2.2. *Equality test for asset and equity volatility and the interpretation of results*

The averages of share and asset volatilities are, respectively, 28% and 22%. A difference in the deviation of six points can be the object of a significance test[9].

Significance between share and asset volatility	Mean	Number of companies	Hypothesis test (threshold: 5%)	
			Test used	Result
σE	0.28	30	Student	Insignificant difference
σV	0.22	30		

Table 3.3. *Differences between the mean asset and equity volatilities (CAC 40)*

This result justifies finding the volatility of assets using the Black–Scholes–Merton method of equity valuation.

3.2.3. *Equality test for growth potential of stock prices based on the approach of brokers and Black–Scholes–Merton and the interpretation of results*

The average of potential growth based on the target value of brokers and on the equity valuation of Black–Scholes–Merton are, respectively, 7.5% and 13.7%. The difference of the deviation of 6.2 points can be the object of a significance test[10].

The difference between the respective approaches of brokers and Black–Scholes–Merton corresponds to the amount of net debt that is taken from the company value obtained via the DCF method. The justification of such a result resides in the fact that companies in the CAC 40 index are in a healthy financial state. Thus, their bankruptcy risk is very low, close to 0%. In this case, $\Phi(-d_2) = 0$ which means that $\Phi(d_2) = 1$ when $d_2 = +\infty$. Therefore,

9 See Appendix 23 and Appendix 9.

10 See Appendix 23 and Appendix 11.

$d_1 = +\infty$ as well, which implies that $\Phi(d_1) = 1$. Using the Black–Scholes–Merton formula as a basis: $E = EV - D.e^{-r\tau}$. Since τ is relatively low, the value of equity is close to that of $EV - D$. The justification of the equal growth potentials can be completed by a statistical equality test of the debt ratios, which corresponds to the relationship between net debt and company value.

Significance between the growth potential of stock prices using the DCF and real options methods	Mean	Number of Companies	Hypothesis test (threshold: 5%)	
			Test used	Result
g brokers	0.075	30	Student	Insignificant difference
g BSM	0.137	30		

Table 3.4. *Difference between the mean growth potentials of stock prices using the DCF and real options methods (CAC 40)*

3.2.4. *Equality test for debt ratios based on net debt from the financial states of companies and the recalculation of net debt using the Black–Scholes–Merton approach, and the interpretation of results*

The average debt ratios based on the target values of brokers and on the equity valuation method by Black–Scholes–Merton are, respectively, 25% and 18.5%. The deviation of 6.5 points can be the object of a significance test[11].

Significance between the debt ratios based on accounting and economic values of debt	Mean	Number of companies	Hypothesis test (threshold: 5%)	
			Test used	Result
D/EV	0.25	30	Aspin Welch	Insignificant difference
B/EV	0.185	30		

Table 3.5. *Difference between the mean debt ratios based on accounting and economic net debt (CAC 40)*

11 See Appendix 23 and Appendix 13.

This result allows us to confirm the relevance of using the economic debt in the real options approach.

3.2.5. *Regression coefficient to explain growth potential of stock prices*

Let us suppose that g is the growth potential of stock prices, *RRGD* is the recovery rate given default, *D/EV* is the net accounting debt on the company value and τ is the maturity of the financial debt. Table 3.7 below shows that

$$g = 2.08.\text{RRGD} - 0.85.\text{D/EV} + 0.05.\tau - 0.47$$

The coefficient of determination, R^2, is approximately 0.8, which is high, but this regression is only significant if the four coefficients are significantly different from 0. Table 3.6 below allows us to test whether the four coefficients are simultaneously equal to 0. According to these hypotheses, $RRGD = D/EV = \tau = 0$, "*F stat*" follows a Fisher–Snedecor distribution F (*k*; *n-k-1*) with $k = 3$ and $n = 28$. Therefore, $F \rightarrow F(3;24)$. The Fisher–Snedecor table gives: P [F > 3.01] = 5%. In other words, if the four coefficients are simultaneously equal to 0, F has a 5% chance of being higher than 3.01. Empirically, $t^* = 34.62 > 3.01$. Thus, with an error risk of 5%, the four coefficients are not simultaneously equal to 0.

	Degree of freedom	**Sum of squares**	**Mean of squares**	**F**	**Critical value of F**
Regression	3	1.14	0.38	34.62	0.00
Residual figures	24	0.26	0.01		
Total	27	1.41			

Table 3.6. *Analysis of the variance (CAC 40)*

Table 3.7 allows us to test if each coefficient a is equal to 0. If $a = 0$, T stat obeys a Student distribution with *n-k-1* degrees of freedom. Here, $k = 3$ and $n = 28$. Thus, $T \rightarrow S(24)$. The Fisher–Snedecor table allows us to obtain P [-2.06 < T < 2.06] = 95%. In other words, if a coefficient is equal to 0, T has a 95% chance of finding itself in the interval [-2.06; 2.06]. Through experimentation:

$t^*(c) = -5.76 < -2.06$, where c is a constant, $t^*(RRGD) = 4.71 > 2.06$.

$t^*(D/EV) = -2.44 < -2.06$, $t^*(t) = 3.51 > 2.06$. Hence, with an error risk of 5%, none of the four coefficients is equal to 0.

	Coefficients	**Error type**	**t stat = t***	**Probability**	**Inferior limit for a confidence threshold = 95%**	**Superior limit for a confidence threshold = 95%**
Constant	-0.47	0.08	-5.76	0.00	-0.64	-0.30
RR GD	2.08	0.44	4.71	0.00	1.17	2.99
D/EV	-0.85	0.35	-2.44	0.02	-1.58	-0.13
t	0.05	0.01	3.51	0.00	0.02	0.07

Table 3.7. *Regression coefficient (CAC 40)*

3.3. Application to a business sector: the cinema industry

Using the data from Facset and in the reference documents of the companies in the sample, the empirical studies carried out focus on the valuation of companies in the cinema sector using the real options and DCF methods. The analysis of this sector seems useful given the disparities in terms of financial structures and the level of development among the selected companies. After the evaluation of potential growth in stock prices using the chosen methods of valuation, the objective is to study, in particular, the differences in significance between them in order to arrive at a conclusion regarding the relevance and reliability of real options when faced with heterogeneous situations. In this context, it turns out that the two methods reveal, on average, equal differences in significance between the growth potentials of stock prices and between the debt ratios based on the economic value of the debt, on the one hand, and its accounting value, on the other.

3.3.1. *Databases, methodology and hypotheses*

In order to carry out statistical tests on a business sector, Heller and Levyne (2016)[12] initially selected 22 companies in the cinema industry. For each company in the sample, the market capitalization, the consensus of

12 Heller, D. and Levyne, O. (2016). Cinema industry: Usefulness of the real options approach for valuation purpose. *International Journal of Business*, 21(1), 26–41.

brokers on the value of the company (arrived at via the DCF method) and on the target value of equity were taken from the Facset financial database on April 3, 2015. Then, the volatility of shares was calculated. Each of the daily volatilities of the last two years was multiplied by $\sqrt{258}$ in order to annualize them. To get homogeneous elements, the Cineplex, Cineworld, Europacorp and Mediaset data were converted into dollars. The exchange rates use on April 3, 2015 were the following:

– EUR = 1.1129 USD (data converted for Europacorp and Mediaset);

– USD = 1.2519 CAD (data converted for Cineplex);

– GBP = 1.534 USD (data converted for Cineworld).

The lack of information on the consensus of brokers led to the exclusion of five companies initially present in the sample: BAC Majestic, Gaumont SA, IMAX Corporation, Reading International Inc and Xilam Animation SA. Thus, the empirical studies concentrate on a sample set of 17 companies.

The potential for growth from the brokers was calculated by relating the target value of equity (obtained through the DCF method) to the daily market capitalization, and then subtracting 1. The risk-free rates in continuous time[13] were obtained by considering the OAT rates of the countries of origin of each company – rates with the same maturity as the average repayment maturity of the company debt in question.

For example, after calculations, the average maturity of debt repayment of Carmike is 9.8 years. Thus, the risk-free rate for this American company was 0.54% – a tax corresponding to the OAT rate for the USA at 10 years on April 3, 2015 (the day that the stock data was collected). It turns out that sometimes, the country that the company comes from does not have a maturity for the debt to be repaid (beyond an OAT rate) corresponding to the same average maturity on the company's debt. Thus, the risk-free rate used was closer to this initial maturity. For example, the United States did not issue Treasury Bills at nine years. Hence, the risk-free rate used for a company like Viacom, whose average repayment maturity for the debt nominal is 9.2 years, was the one corresponding to the OAT rate for the United States at 10 years, or 0.54%.

13 ln (1+ r), where r is the risk-free rate.

The exercise price, moreover, is equal to the amount of accounting debt found in the reference documents of each company at the end of business 2013. To apply the real options valuation method, two other parameters had to be figured: the average residual maturity and the volatility of assets, that is, the volatility of the company value. As in the previous study, the estimation of the company value and its volatility were based on the methodology proposed by Hull *et al.* (2005)[14]. The latter relies on the resolution of a system using the Excel calculator[15].

The empirical studies therefore focus on the potential for growth in stock prices of a sample set of companies in the cinema industry. It is based on the target values established by brokers using the DCF method and the values obtained via the real options approach compared, systematically, to the market capitalization on the day of the evaluation. The Black–Scholes–Merton approach considers the bankruptcy risk of companies through the integration of debt maturity and asset volatility.

The net debt should therefore not be overestimated since it relies on an economic value. Because of this, the model should demonstrate the growth potential of the economic value of equity thanks to the new division of the company value.

The difference between these two growth potentials can be justified by observing the financial leverage calculated using the accounting net debt D or the economic net debt B.

Given the preceding results regarding the CAC 40 stock index, it seemed pertinent to examine one business sector in particular that is made up of more heterogeneous companies in terms of evolution perspectives and the level of risk especially. In this way, the utility of this study is to consider the same hypotheses for the results that will be obtained compared with the preceding study, knowing the significant differences presented above. The hypotheses in question are as follows:

– the differences of significance between the volatility of shares and that of assets should be equal, allowing us to justify the inclusion of asset

14 Hull, J.C., Nelken, I., White, A. (2005). Merton's model, credit risk and volatility skews. *Journal of Credit Risk*, 1(1), 3–28.

15 See Appendix 15 and Appendix 16.

volatility (instead of share volatility) in the real options valuation method in a sector where the differences are noteworthy;

– the differences of significance between the percentage of evolution of stock prices for the companies in the sample using the DCF and the real options methods should be different within a sector where analyst forecasts can be less reliable than for companies in the CAC 40;

– the differences of significance between the debt ratios based on the accounting net debt, on the one hand, and the economic value (obtained using the Black–Scholes–Merton method), on the other, should be equal, allowing us to justify the use of economic debt.

3.3.2. *Equality test for volatility of assets and equity and interpretation of results*

The averages of share and asset volatilities are, respectively, 31% and 25%. The difference of the deviation of six points can be the object of a significance test[16].

Significance between share and asset volatilities	Mean	Number of companies	Hypothesis test (threshold: 5%)	
			Test used	Result
σE	0.31	17	Student	Insignificant difference
σV	0.25	17		

Table 3.8. *Differences between mean asset and equity volatilities (cinema)*

This result justifies determining the volatility of assets using the equity valuation method by Black–Scholes–Merton.

3.3.3. *Equality test for the growth potential of stock prices based on the approach of brokers and Black–Scholes–Merton*

The average potential growth based on the target value of brokers and on the valuation of equity by Black–Scholes–Merton are, respectively, 17.5%

16 See Appendix 23 and Appendix 17.

and 3.8%. The difference in the deviation of 13.7 points can be the object of a significance test[17].

Significance between growth potential of stock prices using the DCF and real options methods	Mean	Number of companies	Hypothesis test (threshold: 5%)	
			Test used	Result
g brokers	0.175	17	Aspin Welch	Insignificant difference
g BSM	0.038	17		

Table 3.9. *Difference between the mean growth potentials of stock prices using the DCF and real options methods (cinema)*

The forecasts of brokers for this business sector are reliable. In other words, their forecasts, especially regarding the level of risk, are coherent. The approach using real options does not bring about a better valuation and is just as relevant as the DCF method.

The justification of the equal growth potentials can be completed by a statistical test for the equal debt ratios which corresponds to the net debt/company value.

3.3.4. *Test for equal debt ratios based on net debt from the financial reports of companies and the recalculation of net debts using the Black–Scholes–Merton approach*

The averages of debt ratios based on the target values of brokers and on the equity valuation method by Black–Scholes–Merton are, respectively, 21.5% and 19.5%. The deviation of two points can be the object of a significance test[18].

17 See Appendix 23 and Appendix 19.

18 See Appendix 23 and Appendix 21.

Significance between debt ratios based on the accounting and economic values of the debt	Mean	Number of companies	Hypothesis test (threshold: 5%)	
			Test used	Result
D/EV	0.215	17	Student	Insignificant difference
B/EV	0.195	17		

Table 3.10. *Difference between the mean debt ratios based on accounting net and economic debt (cinema)*

This result allows us to confirm the relevance of using the economic net debt in the real options approach for the cinema industry.

Conclusion

Real options allow for valuation of the structure of liabilities. Analogously with financial options, equity resembles the purchase of a call, and net debt can be assimilated to the sale of a put. The shareholders thus hold a "real" call over the economic assets of the company. On the date of maturity of the debt, they either exercise it and repay it, or they abandon it and abandon the company to creditors.

The value of this call thus represents the economic value of company equity. From the point of view of the creditor, loaning funds to a company comes down to investing in the risk-free assets and giving the shareholder a "real" option to sell of the economic assets at an exercise price that is equal to the amount of debt to repay. Creditors can therefore become the owners of the economic assets if the company goes bankrupt, that is, if it doesn't acquit itself of its debt. Indeed, unless they recover the amount of loaned funds, they recover the economic assets that they purchased for an amount of debt that is not repaid to them. The sale of this put is a supplementary retribution for the creditor which adds to the risk-free rate to constitute the total remuneration. The creditor risks the put being exercised by shareholders, that is, the company will not respect its agreements.

The value of this option is equal to the difference between the value of the loan discounted at the risk-free rate and the market value of this loan discounted at an interest rate that takes the risk of non-repayment into account, that is, the cost of the debt. This is the risk premium that exists for any loan with respect to a risk-free loan.

Traditionally, to evaluate the equity of a company, analysts use the DCF method. Besides the aforementioned critiques regarding the subjectivity of the hypotheses, the net debt, which is deducted from the value of the company to obtain the value of equity, should ideally also be based on its economic value. Thus, real options can be a complementary approach because of the inclusion of the economic net debt, its maturity, the evaluated probability that the company will go bankrupt and the volatility of its assets. The optional references, that is, principally Black–Scholes (1973), Merton (1974) and Hull *et al.* (2005), therefore propose a new company value that is understood to be between the economic value of equity and also that of the net debt, considering the volatility of assets (and not that of shares).

Appendices

Appendix 1

Partial Derivatives in the Option Price Equation by Galaï and Masulis (1976)

$$S = VN(d_1) - Ce^{-rf.T}N(d_2) > 0 \qquad [A1.1]$$

$$S_V \equiv \frac{\partial S}{\partial V} = N(d_1) > 0 \qquad [A1.2]$$

$$S_C \equiv \frac{\partial S}{\partial C} = -e^{-rf.T}N(d_2) < 0 \qquad [A1.3]$$

$$S_{\sigma^2} \equiv \frac{\partial S}{\partial \sigma^2} = Ce^{-rf.T}Z(d_2)\frac{\sqrt{T}}{2\sigma} > 0 \qquad [A1.4]$$

$$S_{r_f} \equiv \frac{\partial S}{\partial r_f} = TC\,e^{-rf.T}N(d_2) > 0 \qquad [A1.5]$$

$$S_T \equiv \frac{\partial S}{\partial T} = C\,e^{-r_f T}r_f N(d_2) + C\,e^{-r_f T}Z(d_2)\frac{\sigma}{2\sqrt{T}} > 0 \qquad [A1.6]$$

with:

$$Z(d_1) = \frac{1}{\sqrt{2\pi}}\,e^{-\frac{d_1^2}{2}}$$

where $Z(d_1)$ is the density of the standard distribution in d_1.

Appendix 2

Partial Derivatives for Systematic Risk of Company Debt by Galaï and Masulis (1976)

The partial derivatives for the systematic risk of the debt when the company's systematic risk is stable and positive (i.e. $\frac{\partial \beta_V}{\partial K} = 0$ and $\beta_V > 0$) are as follows:

$$R \equiv \frac{VN(-d_1)Ce^{-r_f T}N(d_2)}{D^2\sigma\sqrt{T}} \qquad [A2.1]$$

$$\frac{\partial \beta_D}{\partial V} = -\frac{R}{V}\left[\frac{Z(-d_1)}{N(-d_1)} + \frac{Z(d_2)}{N(d_2)} - \sigma\sqrt{T}\right]\beta_V < 0 \qquad [A2.2]$$

$$\frac{\partial \beta_D}{\partial C} = -\frac{R}{C}\left[\frac{Z(-d_1)}{N(-d_1)} + \frac{Z(d_2)}{N(d_2)} - \sigma\sqrt{T}\right]\beta_V > 0 \qquad [A2.3]$$

$$\frac{\partial \beta_D}{\partial r_f} = -RT\left[\frac{Z(-d_1)}{N(-d_1)} + \frac{Z(d_2)}{N(d_2)} - \sigma\sqrt{T}\right]\beta_V < 0 \qquad [A2.4]$$

$$\frac{\partial \beta_D}{\partial \sigma^2} = -\frac{R\sqrt{T}}{2\sigma}\left[d_2\frac{Z(-d_1)}{N(-d_1)} + d_1\frac{Z(d_2)}{N(d_2)}\right]\beta_V \begin{cases} \geq 0 \\ \leq 0 \end{cases} \qquad [A2.5]$$

$$\frac{\partial \beta_D}{\partial T} = R\left[-r_f\left(\frac{Z(-d_1)}{N(-d_1)} + \frac{Z(d_2)}{N(d_2)} - \sigma\sqrt{T}\right) + \frac{\sigma}{2\sqrt{T}}\left(d_2\frac{Z(-d_1)}{N(-d_1)} + d_1\frac{Z(d_2)}{N(d_2)}\right)\right]\beta_V \begin{cases} \geq 0 \\ \leq 0 \end{cases} \qquad [A2.6]$$

with:

$$\frac{Z(-d_1)}{N(-d_1)} + \frac{Z(d_2)}{N(d_2)} - \sigma\sqrt{T} > 0 \qquad [A2.7]$$

$$d_2 \frac{Z(-d_1)}{N(-d_1)} + d_1 \frac{Z(d_2)}{N(d_2)} \begin{cases} \geq 0 \\ \leq 0 \end{cases} \qquad [A2.8]$$

and:

$$Z(d_1) = Z(-d_1) \qquad [A2.9]$$

Appendix 3

Partial Derivatives for Systematic Risk of Company Equity by Galaï and Masulis (1976)

The partial derivatives of the systematic risk of equity when the systematic risk of the company is stable and positive (i.e. $\frac{\partial \beta_V}{\partial K} = 0$ and $\beta_V > 0$) are as follows:

$$Q \equiv \frac{VN(d_1)Ce^{-r_f T}N(d_2)}{S^2 \sigma \sqrt{T}} > 0, \qquad [A3.1]$$

$$\frac{\partial \beta_S}{\partial V} = -\frac{Q}{V}\left[\frac{Z(d_1)}{N(d_1)} - \frac{Z(d_2)}{N(d_2)} + \sigma\sqrt{T}\right]\beta_V < 0 \qquad [A3.2]$$

$$\frac{\partial \beta_S}{\partial C} = \frac{Q}{C}\left[\frac{Z(d_1)}{N(d_1)} - \frac{Z(d_2)}{N(d_2)} + \sigma\sqrt{T}\right]\beta_V > 0 \qquad [A3.3]$$

$$\frac{\partial \beta_S}{\partial r_f} = -QT\left[\frac{Z(d_1)}{N(d_1)} - \frac{Z(d_2)}{N(d_2)} + \sigma\sqrt{T}\right]\beta_V < 0 \qquad [A3.4]$$

$$\frac{\partial \beta_S}{\partial \sigma^2} = -\frac{Q\sqrt{T}}{2\sigma}\left[d_1\frac{Z(d_2)}{N(d_2)} - d_2\frac{Z(d_1)}{N(d_1)}\right]\beta_V < 0 \qquad [A3.5]$$

$$\frac{\partial \beta_S}{\partial T} = -Q.$$

$$\left[r_f\left(\frac{Z(d_1)}{N(d_1)} - \frac{Z(d_2)}{N(d_2)} + \sigma\sqrt{T}\right) + \frac{\sigma}{2\sqrt{T}}\left(d_1\frac{Z(d_2)}{N(d_2)} - d_2\frac{Z(d_1)}{N(d_1)}\right)\right]\beta_V < 0 \qquad [A3.6]$$

with:

$$d_1 \frac{Z(d_2)}{N(d_2)} - d_2 \frac{Z(d_1)}{N(d_1)} > 0 \quad \text{[A3.7]}$$

$$\frac{Z(d_1)}{N(d_1)} - \frac{Z(d_2)}{N(d_2)} + \sigma\sqrt{T} > 0 \quad \text{[A3.8]}$$

and:

$$VZ(d_1) = Ce^{-rfT}Z(d_2) \quad \text{[A3.9]}$$

Appendix 4

Proof of Inequalities by Galaï and Masulis (1976)

In using the Mill ratio[1], we assert that

$$\frac{\mathrm{Z(d)}}{\mathrm{N(d)}} > -d, for -\infty < d < \infty \qquad [A4.1]$$

With the previous inequality, we can deduce that, for inequality [A2.7]:

$$\frac{\mathrm{Z}(-\mathrm{d}_1)}{\mathrm{N}(-\mathrm{d}_1)} + \frac{\mathrm{Z}(\mathrm{d}_2)}{\mathrm{N}(\mathrm{d}_2)} - \sigma\sqrt{\mathrm{T}} > \mathrm{d}_1 - \mathrm{d}_2 - \sigma\sqrt{\mathrm{T}} = 0 \qquad [A4.2]$$

By transforming inequality [A2.8], we see that:

$$\mathrm{d}_2 \frac{\mathrm{Z}(-\mathrm{d}_1)}{\mathrm{N}(-\mathrm{d}_1)} + \mathrm{d}_1 \frac{\mathrm{Z}(\mathrm{d}_2)}{\mathrm{N}(\mathrm{d}_2)}$$

$$= \left[\mathrm{d}_2\mathrm{Ce}^{-\mathrm{rfT}}\mathrm{N}(\mathrm{d}_2) + \mathrm{d}_1\mathrm{VN}(-\mathrm{d}_1)\right] \times \left[\mathrm{Ce}^{-\mathrm{rfT}}\mathrm{N}(\mathrm{d}_2)(\mathrm{Z}(-\mathrm{d}_1))^{-1}\mathrm{N}(-\mathrm{d}_1)\right]^{-1}$$

$$= \left[\mathrm{d}_1\mathrm{D} - \sigma\sqrt{\mathrm{T}}\,\mathrm{Ce}^{-\mathrm{rfT}}\mathrm{N}(\mathrm{d}_2)\right] \times \left[\mathrm{Ce}^{-\mathrm{rfT}}\mathrm{N}(\mathrm{d}_2)(\mathrm{Z}(-\mathrm{d}_1))^{-1}\mathrm{N}(-\mathrm{d}_1)\right]^{-1} \begin{cases} \geq 0 \\ \leq 0 \end{cases} \qquad [A4.3]$$

1 Gordon, R.D. (1941). Values of Mill's ratio of area to bounding ordinate and of the normal probability integral for large values of the arguments. *Annals of Mathematical Statistics*, 12, 364–366.

when:

$$d_1 \begin{cases} \geq \\ \leq \end{cases} \sigma\sqrt{T}\,\frac{Ce^{-rfT}N(d_2)}{D} \text{ and with } 0 \leq \frac{Ce^{-rfT}N(d_2)}{D} \leq 1$$

Therefore, expression [A2.8] is always superior to 0 for $d_1 > \sigma\sqrt{T}$ or $V > Ce^{-(rf+\frac{\sigma^2}{2})T}$.

By transforming inequality [A3.7], we find that:

$$d_1\frac{Z(d_2)}{N(d_2)} - d_2\frac{Z(d_1)}{N(d_1)}$$

$$= \left[d_1VN(d_1) - d_2Ce^{-rfT}N(d_2)\right] \times [Ce^{-rfT}N(d_2)(Z(d_1))^{-1}N(d_1)]^{-1}$$

$$= \left[d_1S + \sigma\sqrt{T}\,Ce^{-rfT}N(d_2)\right] \times [Ce^{-rfT}N(d_2)(Z(d_1))^{-1}N(d_1)]^{-1} \qquad [A4.4]$$

This relationship will be positive if:

$$d_1 > -\sigma\sqrt{T}\,\frac{Ce^{-rfT}N(d_2)}{S} \text{ with } \frac{Ce^{-rfT}N(d_2)}{S} \geq 0$$

Because of this, [A3.7] will always be positive for companies when $V \geq Ce^{-\left(rf+\frac{\sigma^2}{2}\right)T}$ (the value of company assets is at least equal to the discounted nominal value of its debt) or likewise, when $d_1 \geq 0$.

By defining $h(d) \equiv \frac{Z(d)}{N(d)} + d$, we know that h(d) is always positive. We can demonstrate that h'(d) > 0 regardless of the value of d. This means that h(d) is a monotonic function of d and strictly a growth function. If $d_1 > d_2$, then $h(d_1) - h(d_2) > 0$.

Given that $d_2 = d_1 - \sigma\sqrt{T}$, we can deduce that for inequality [A3.8]:

$$\frac{Z(d_1)}{N(d_1)} - \frac{Z(d_2)}{N(d_2)} + \sigma\sqrt{T} = \left(\frac{Z(d_1)}{N(d_1)} + d_1\right) - \left(\frac{Z(d_2)}{N(d_2)} + d_2\right) = h(d_1) - h(d_2) > 0 \qquad [A4.5]$$

Appendix 5

Partial Derivatives in the Option Price Equation by Bellalah and Jacquillat (1995)

$$S = Ve^{(\lambda_V - \lambda_S)T} N(d_1) - Ee^{-(r+\lambda_S)T} N(d_2) > 0, \quad [A5.1]$$

$$\frac{\partial S}{\partial V} = e^{(\lambda_V - \lambda_S)T} N(d_1) > 0 \text{ (even between 0 and 1)} \quad [A5.2]$$

$$\frac{\partial S}{\partial E} = -\,Ee^{-(r+\lambda_S).T} N(d_2) < 0, \quad [A5.3]$$

$$\frac{\partial S}{\partial \sigma^2} = Ee^{-(r+\lambda_S)T} \sqrt{T}\, n(d_2) > 0, \quad [A5.4]$$

$$\frac{\partial S}{\partial r} = TE\, e^{-(r+\lambda_S)T} N(d_2) > 0, \quad [A5.5]$$

$$\frac{\partial S}{\partial T} = (\lambda_V - \lambda_S)Ve^{(\lambda_V - \lambda_S)T} N(d_1) + (r + \lambda_S)E\, e^{-(r+\lambda_S)T} N(d_2)$$
$$+E\, e^{-(r+\lambda_S)T}\, n(d2)\frac{\sigma}{2\sqrt{T}} > 0 \quad [A5.6]$$

$n(d_2) = \frac{1}{\sqrt{2\pi}}\, e^{-\frac{d_1^2}{2}}$ where $n(d_2)$ is the density of the standard distribution in d_2.

Appendix 6

Characteristics of Companies in the CAC 40

Company	Market capitalization (February 22, 2013)	Target value of equity (DCF)	Broker consensus company value	Broker growth potential	Share volatility
Accor S.A.	6,414	6,599	7,074	3%	29%
Air Liquide S.A.	28,942	31,507	34,666	9%	20%
Alstrom S.A.	10,170	10,846	12,777	7%	36%
ArcelorMittal S.A.	19,185	23,427	33,957	22%	39%
Bouygues S.A.	6,517	7,362	11,541	13%	32%
Carrefour S.A.	14,894	15,209	20,306	2%	33%
Compagnie St-Gobain	16,720	18,169	24,221	9%	34%
Danone S.A.	33,932	32,517	39,300	-4%	21%
Electricité de France S.A.	27,030	29,788	67,684	10%	28%
Essilor International S.A.	16,261	16,381	16,356	1%	20%
France Telecom	19,922	26,652	51,448	34%	27%
GDF Suez S.A.	35,444	41,789	79,613	18%	25%
Gemalto N.V.	6,001	6,197	5,567	3%	28%
Lafarge S.A.	14,114	14,891	24,324	6%	33%
LeGrand S.A.	9,229	8,398	10,157	-9%	23%
LVMH	67,241	77,707	70,663	16%	26%

Company	Market capitalization (February 22, 2013)	Target value of equity (DCF)	Broker consensus company value	Broker growth potential	Share volatility
Michelin	12,124	14,427	13,998	19%	31%
Pernod Ricard S.A.	25,969	25,025	33,425	-4%	19%
PPR S.A.	21,635	20,855	22,942	-4%	25%
Publicis Groupe S.A.	10,601	10,151	10,372	-4%	19%
Safran S.A.	14,260	15,000	15,092	5%	24%
Sanofi S.A.	96,611	103,893	103,138	8%	22%
Schneider Electric S.A.	32,727	31,138	35,684	-5%	34%
Solvay S.A.	9,292	9,454	12,156	2%	33%
Total S.A.	90,047	105,145	108,524	17%	21%
Unibail-Rodamco SE	16,464	16,812	28,495	2%	20%
Vallourec S.A.	5,291	5,000	6,653	-6%	41%
Veolia Environnement S.A.	4,774	5,472	17,728	15%	39%
Vinci S.A.	20,640	25,363	33,963	23%	28%
Viviendi	20,449	24,258	34,146	19%	30%

Table A6.1.

Appendix 7

Valuation of Companies in the CAC 40 Using the Black–Scholes–Merton Method

The following table groups together the results of the calculations, making it possible to obtain all the parameters of the Black–Scholes formula in order to determine the economic value of equity using the real options method.

Company	Broker consensus EV	Risk-free rate in %	Share volatility in %	Accounting debt	Cash flow and equiv.	Net debt	Average maturity	d1	d2	Φ(d1) in %	Φ(d2) in %	Φ(-d1) in %	Φ(-d2) in %	Econ. value of debt	Net debt in %EV	Econ. value of E	B&S growth potential in %
Accor S.A.	7,074	2.18%	29%	1,717	1,491	226	3.4	3.09	2.57	100	99	0	1	101	1	6,974	9
Air Liquide S.A.	34,666	2.18%	20%	7,036	1,788	5,248	4.7	4.65	4.27	100	100	0	0	4,563	13	30,103	4
Alstrom S.A.	12,777	2.18%	36%	4,466	3,180	1,286	4.5	2.02	1.34	98	91	2	9	776	6	12,001	18
ArcelorMittal S.A.	33,957	2.18%	39%	20,020	2,959	17,060	6.3	1.39	0.77	92	78	8	22	13,459	40	20,498	7
Bouygues S.A.	11,541	2.18%	32%	7,023	3,161	3,862	7.3	1.37	0.76	92	78	8	22	2,469	21	9,072	39
Carrefour S.A.	20,306	2.18%	33%	11,672	4,760	6,912	5.3	1.44	0.85	92	80	8	20	5,119	25	15,187	2
Compagnie St-Gobain	24,221	2.18%	34%	11,044	2,949	8,095	5.8	1.79	1.18	96	88	4	12	6,514	27	17,707	6
Danone S.A.	39,300	2.18%	21%	9,031	2,141	6,890	4.9	4.14	3.74	100	100	0	0	5,973	15	33,328	-2
Electricité de France S.A.	67,684	2.18%	28%	50,286	17,001	33,285	7.9	1.24	0.78	89	78	11	22	23,401	35	44,282	64
Essilor International S.A.	16,356	2.18%	20%	904	397	507	2.5	9.85	9.54	100	100	0	0	459	3	15,897	-2
France Telecom	51,448	2.18%	27%	40,703	10,291	30,412	9.0	1.18	0.73	88	77	12	23	21,512	42	29,936	50
GDF Suez S.A.	79,613	2.18%	25%	56,994	19,394	37,600	11.2	1.37	0.84	91	80	9	20	23,205	29	56,408	59
Gemalto N.V.	5,567	2.18%	28%	504	339	165	1.0	8.88	8.60	100	100	0	0	154	3	5,413	-10
Lafarge S.A.	24,324	2.18%	33%	15,286	3,312	11,974	5.9	1.39	0.87	92	81	8	19	9,542	39	14,782	5
LeGrand S.A.	10,157	2.18%	23%	1,757	488	1,269	8.3	3.57	2.98	100	100	0	0	979	10	9,178	-1
LVMH	70,663	2.18%	26%	7,100	2,303	4,797	6.3	4.33	3.73	100	100	0	0	3,893	6	66,770	-1

Michelin	13,998	2.18%	31%	3,839	2,025	1,814	6.8	2.34	1.61	99	95	1	5	1,242	9	12,756	5
Pernod Ricard S.A.	33,425	2.18%	19%	9,866	828	9,038	5.7	3.81	3.44	100	100	0	0	7,879	24	25,546	-2
PPR S.A.	22,942	2.18%	25%	4,678	1,282	3,396	3.6	4.15	3.72	100	100	0	0	3,045	13	19,897	-8
Publicis Groupe S.A.	10,372	2.18%	19%	2,284	2,174	110	2.8	5.12	4.81	100	100	0	0	(24)	0	10,396	-2
Safran S.A.	15,092	2.18%	24%	2,445	1,448	997	3.4	4.74	4.32	100	100	0	0	824	5	14,268	0
Sanofi S.A.	103,138	2.18%	22%	14,983	4,124	10,859	4.6	4.86	4.43	100	100	0	0	9,435	9	93,703	-3
Schneider Electric S.A.	35,684	2.18%	34%	8,037	2,771	5,266	6.2	2.54	1.79	99	96	1	4	4,190	12	31,494	-4
Solvay S.A.	12,156	2.18%	33%	4,168	2,407	1,761	6.3	2.03	1.30	98	90	2	10	1,135	9	11,021	19
Total S.A.	108,524	2.18%	21%	32,399	16,701	15,698	4.4	3.61	3.22	100	100	0	0	12,722	12	95,802	6
Unibail-Rodamco SE	28,495	2.18%	20%	9,749	162	9,587	4.5	3.81	3.49	100	100	0	0	8,677	30	19,818	20
Vallourec S.A.	6,653	2.18%	41%	2,095	902	1,193	5.5	1.97	1.16	98	88	2	12	888	13	5,765	9
Veolia Environnement S.A.	17,728	2.18%	39%	20,454	5,724	14,730	7.4	0.24	(0.15)	59	44	41	56	9,156	52	8,572	80
Vinci S.A.	33,963	2.18%	28%	20,871	8,281	12,590	9.2	1.42	0.80	92	79	8	21	7,849	23	26,114	27
Viviendi	34,146	2.18%	30%	15,710	3,683	12,027	4.6	2.10	1.63	98	95	2	5	10,397	30	23,749	16

Table A7.1. *Valuations of CAC 40 companies using real options*

Appendix 8

Distribution of Debt Relative to the Rate of Recovery (CAC 40)

Company	B&S growth potential	Recovery rate	D/EV	t	B/EV	Φ(-d2)
Accor S.A.	9%	19%	3%	3.4	1%	1%
Air Liquide S.A.	4%	17%	15%	4.7	13%	0%
Alstrom S.A.	18%	24%	10%	4.5	6%	9%
ArcelorMittal S.A.	7%	38%	50%	6.3	40%	22%
Bouygues S.A.	39%	38%	33%	7.3	21%	22%
Carrefour S.A.	2%	38%	34%	5.3	25%	20%
Compagnie St-Gobain	6%	31%	33%	5.8	27%	12%
Danone S.A.	-2%	19%	18%	4.9	15%	0%
Electricité de France S.A.	64%	49%	49%	7.9	35%	22%
Essilor International S.A.	50%	51%	59%	9.0	42%	23%
France Telecom	59%	43%	47%	11.2	29%	20%
GDF Suez S.A.	5%	43%	49%	5.9	39%	19%
Gemalto N.V.	-1%	12%	12%	8.3	10%	0%
Lafarge S.A.	-1%	8%	7%	6.3	6%	0%
LeGrand S.A.	5%	18%	13%	6.8	9%	5%
LVMH	-2%	24%	27%	5.7	24%	0%
Michelin	-8%	17%	15%	3.6	13%	0%

Company	B&S growth potential	Recovery rate	D/EV	t	B/EV	Φ(-d2)
Pernod Ricard S.A.	-2%	20%	1%	2.8	0%	0%
PPR S.A.	0%	14%	7%	3.4	5%	0%
Publicis Groupe S.A.	-3%	12%	11%	4.6	9%	0%
Safran S.A.	-4%	15%	15%	6.2	12%	4%
Sanofi S.A.	19%	22%	14%	6.3	9%	10%
Schneider Electric S.A.	6%	25%	14%	4.4	12%	0%
Solvay S.A.	20%	29%	34%	4.5	30%	0%
Total S.A.	9%	20%	18%	5.5	13%	12%
Unibail-Rodamco SE	80%	73%	83%	7.4	52%	56%
Vallourec S.A.	27%	37%	37%	9.2	23%	21%
Veolia Environnement S.A.	16%	35%	35%	4.6	30%	5%
Vinci S.A.	9%	19%	3%	3.4	1%	1%
Viviendi	4%	17%	15%	4.7	13%	0%

Table A8.1. *Growth potential and economic debt (CAC 40)*

Appendix 9

F-Equality Test of Variances for Asset and Equity Volatility (CAC 40)

	σ_E	σ_V
Mean	28.0%	22.2%
Variance	0.4%	0.3%
Observations	30	30
Degrees of freedom	29	29
F	1.41	
P(F<=f) unilateral	0.18	
Critical value for F (unilateral)	1.86	

Table A9.1.

Appendix 10

Equality Test for Projected Asset and Equity Volatility (CAC 40): Two Observations with Equal Variations

	σ_E	σ_V
Mean	28.0%	22.2%
Variance	0.4%	0.3%
Observations	30	30
Weighted variance	0.4%	
Hypothetical mean difference	0	
Degrees of freedom	58	
Stat t	3.76	
P(T<=t) bilateral	0.00	
Critical value for F (bilateral)	2.00	

Table A10.1.

Appendix 11

F-Equality Test of Variances for the Growth Potential of Stock Prices Using the DCF and Real Options Methods (CAC 40)

	***g* brokers**	***g* BSM**
Mean	7.5%	13.7%
Variance	1.1%	5.1%
Observations	30	30
Degrees of freedom	29	29
F	0.20	
P(F<=f) unilateral	0.00	
Critical value for F (unilateral)	1.86	

Table A11.1.

Appendix 12

Equality Test for Projected Potential Growth of Stock Prices Using the DCF and Real Options Methods (CAC 40): Two Observations with Equal Variances

	g brokers	*g vs* BSM
Mean	7.5%	13.7%
Variance	1.1%	5.1%
Observations	30	30
Weighted variance	3.1%	
Hypothetical mean difference	0	
Degrees of freedom	58	
Stat t	-1.37	
Critical value for F (bilateral)	2.00	

Table A12.1.

Appendix 13

F-Equality Test of Variances for Debt Ratios Based on an Accounting and Economic Net Debt (CAC 40)

	D/EV	*B/EV*
Mean	25.0%	18.5%
Variance	3.9%	1.9%
Observations	30	30
Degrees of freedom	29	29
F	2.08	0
P(F<=f) unilateral	0.03	0
Critical value for F (unilateral)	1.86	

Table A13.1.

Appendix 14

Equality Test of Projected Debt Ratios Based on an Accounting and Economic Net Debt (CAC 40): Two Observations with Different Variances

	D/EV	*B/EV*
Mean	25.0%	18.5%
Variance	3.9%	1.9%
Observations	30	30
Hypothetical mean difference	0	
Degrees of freedom	52	
Stat t	1.47	
Critical value for F (bilateral)	2.01	

Table A14.1.

Appendix 15

Characteristics of Companies in the Cinema Industry

Company	Market capitalization (April 3, 2015)	Target equity value (DCF)	Broker consensus EV	Broker growth potential	Risk-free rate	Share volatility
21st Century Fox	76,033	86,326	103,993	13.54%	0.54%	21.52%
AMC	3,044	3,119	4,801	2.46%	0.54%	28.11%
Carmike	828	1,039	1,039	25.51%	0.54%	31.32%
CIDM	140	319	546	128.25%	0.12%	53.81%
Cinemark	5,262	5,497	6,840	4.47%	0.54%	19.60%
Cineplex	2,430	2,442	2,691	0.46%	-0.03%	15.74%
Cineworld	1,777	1,750	1,721	-1.53%	0.12%	24.09%
Dreamworks	1,803	1,758	2,346	-2.52%	0.54%	45.30%
Eros	1,014	1,301	1,464	28.32%	-0.03%	41.28%
EuropaCorp	136	178	287	30.53%	-0.01%	40.16%
Lionsgate	4,926	6,120	7,415	24.22%	-0.03%	36.30%
Mediaset	4,780	4,475	5,129	-6.39%	-0.08%	44.49%
RealDInc	704	856	864	21.60%	0.08%	45.46%
Regal	3,446	3,426	5,936	-0.59%	0.30%	18.63%
TimeWarner	77,359	87,125	109,666	12.62%	0.94%	24.09%
Viacom	27,512	31,296	44,919	13.75%	0.54%	19.27%
Walt Disney	195,950	201,142	217,743	2.65%	0.22%	17.99%

Table A15.1.

Company	EV consensus (calculator)	Volatility of assets	Accounting debt	Cash flow and equiv.	Net debt	Net debt in %EV	Average maturity
21st Century Fox	85,251	19.34%	16,458	6,659	9,799	11.49%	11.3
AMC	4,534	20.75%	2,195	546	1,649	36.36%	12.1
Carmike	1,116	24.51%	455	144	311	27.90%	9.8
CIDM	311	31.79%	263	57	206	66.25%	5.7
Cinemark	6,620	16.24%	2,049	600	1,449	21.89%	11.9
Cineplex	2,584	14.83%	190	35	154	5.97%	3.7
Cineworld	1,945	22.12%	198	29	169	8.71%	5.5
Dreamworks	1,977	41.33%	300	95	205	10.35%	12.5
Eros	1,150	36.70%	246	110	136	11.83%	3.7
EuropaCorp	258	27.00%	192	70	122	47.30%	1.2
Lionsgate	5,722	31.73%	858	62	796	13.90%	3.8
Mediaset	6,395	35.33%	1,840	220	1,620	25.34%	3.2
RealDInc	720	44.41%	48	31	16	2.29%	2.5
Regal	5,429	13.76%	2,311	281	2,030	37.39%	7.6
TimeWarner	93,263	20.39%	20,165	1,862	18,303	19.63%	14.3
Viacom	36,532	15.54%	11,885	2,403	9,482	25.96%	9.2
Walt Disney	206,140	17.12%	14,288	3,931	10,357	5.02%	7.4

Table A15.2.

Appendix 16

Valuation of Companies in the Cinema Industry Using the Black–Scholes–Merton Method

Company	d1	d2	F(d1)	F(d2)	F(-d1)	F(-d2)	Econ. value of debt	Econ. net debt in %EV	Econ. value of equity	B&S growth potential
21st Century Fox	2.947	2.296	0.998	0.989	0.002	0.011	8,795	10%	76,456	0.56%
AMC	1.456	0.734	0.927	0.769	0.073	0.231	1,364	30%	3,170	4.14%
Carmike	1.620	0.851	0.947	0.803	0.053	0.197	261	23%	855	3.22%
CIDM	0.609	-0.151	0.729	0.440	0.271	0.560	142	46%	169	20.78%
Cinemark	2.489	1.929	0.994	0.973	0.006	0.027	1,313	20%	5,307	0.87%
Cineplex	9.354	9.071	1.000	1.000	0.000	0.000	154	6%	2,430	-0.02%
Cineworld	4.677	4.158	1.000	1.000	0.000	0.000	168	9%	1,777	-0.02%
Dreamworks	2.067	0.606	0.981	0.728	0.019	0.272	147	7%	1,830	1.48%
Eros	2.532	1.824	0.994	0.966	0.006	0.034	135	12%	1,016	0.19%
EuropaCorp	1.148	0.854	0.874	0.803	0.126	0.197	117	45%	141	3.70%
Lionsgate	3.364	2.743	1.000	0.997	0.000	0.003	796	14%	4,926	0.00%
Mediaset	2.294	1.667	0.989	0.952	0.011	0.048	1,607	25%	4,788	0.16%
RealDInc	4.212	3.507	1.000	1.000	0.000	0.000	16	2%	704	0.03%
Regal	2.502	2.123	0.994	0.983	0.006	0.017	1,973	36%	3,455	0.26%
TimeWarner	2.545	1.775	0.995	0.962	0.005	0.038	15,617	17%	77,646	0.37%
Viacom	2.724	2.253	0.997	0.988	0.003	0.012	8,888	24%	27,644	0.48%
Walt Disney	6.006	5.541	1.000	1.000	0.000	0.000	10,127	5%	196,013	0.03%

Table A16.1.

Appendix 17

F-Equality Test of Variances for Asset and Equity Volatility (Cinema)

	σ_E	σ_V
Mean	31.0%	25.0%
Variance	1.5%	0.9%
Observations	17	17
Degrees of freedom	16	16
F	1.61	
P(F<=f) unilateral	0.17	
Critical value for F (unilateral)	2.33	

Table A17.1.

Appendix 18

Equality Test for Projected Asset and Equity Volatility (Cinema): Two Observations with Equal Variances

	σ_E	σ_V
Mean	31.0%	25.0%
Variance	1.5%	0.9%
Observations	17	17
Weighted variance	1.2%	
Hypothetical mean difference	0	
Degrees of freedom	32	
Stat t	1.60	
P(T<=t) bilateral	0.12	
Critical value for F (bilateral)	2.04	

Table A18.1.

Appendix 19

F-Equality Test for Potential Growth of Stock Prices Using the DCF and Real Options Methods (Cinema)

	g brokers	*g* BSM
Mean	17.5%	3.8%
Variance	9.6%	0.9%
Observations	17	17
Degrees of freedom	16	16
F	10.62	
P(F<=f) unilateral	0.00	
Critical value for F (unilateral)	2.33	

Table A19.1.

Appendix 20

Equality Test for Projected Potential Growth of Stock Prices Using the DCF and Real Options Methods (Cinema): Two Observations with Different Variances

	g brokers	*g* BSM
Mean	17.5%	3.8%
Variance	9.6%	0.9%
Observations	17	17
Hypothetical mean difference	0	
Degrees of freedom	19	
Stat t	1.74	
P(T<=t) bilateral	0.10	
Critical value for F (bilateral)	2.09	

Table A20.1.

Appendix 21

F-Equality Test of Variances for Debt Ratios Based on an Accounting and Economic Net Debt (Cinema)

	D/EV	*B/EV*
Mean	21.5%	19.5%
Variance	2.4%	1.9%
Observations	17	17
Degrees of freedom	16	16
F	1.30	
P(F<=f) unilateral	0.30	
Critical value for F (unilateral)	2.33	

Table A21.1.

Appendix 22

Equality Test for Projected Debt Ratios Based on an Account and Economic Net Debt (Cinema): Two Observations with Equal Variances

	D/EV	*B/EV*
Mean	21.5%	19.5%
Variance	2.4%	1.9%
Observations	17	17
Weighted variance	2.1%	
Hypothetical mean difference	0	
Degrees of freedom	32	
Stat t	0.41	
P(T<=t) bilateral	0.69	
Critical value for F (bilateral)	2.04	

Table A22.1.

Appendix 23

Significance Test for the Difference Between Two Standard Deviations

In order to complete each significance test between traditional valuation methods and using real options, two steps were made:

– The first step consists of completing a variance equality test or F-Test on Excel in order to test the significance of a difference between two standard deviations. Two samples with sizes n_P and n_Q, coming from large populations, have standard respective variances S_x^2 and S_Y^2. Let σ_P^2 and σ_Q^2 be the respective variances of the two total populations and the accepted principle:

$$\frac{S_X^2}{S_Y^2} \cdot \frac{\sigma_Q^2}{\sigma_P^2} \rightarrow F(n_P - 1; n_Q - 1) \qquad [A23.1]$$

where F corresponds to the Fisher–Snedecor law. Let us test the hypothesis $\sigma_P^2 = \sigma_Q^2$. Thus:

$$\frac{\sigma_Q^2}{\sigma_P^2} = 1 \qquad [A23.2]$$

and, if $\sigma_P^2 = \sigma_Q^2$, then:

$$\frac{S_X^2}{S_Y^2} \rightarrow F(n_P - 1; n_Q - 1) \qquad [A23.3]$$

From these samples, we calculate $\frac{S_X^2}{S_Y^2} = t_0^*$. The tabulation of the inverse spread function of the Fisher–Snedecor law allows us to get the real t such that P[T < t] = 95%.

Therefore, if $t_0^* < t$, we have a 95% chance of being right (or a 5% chance of being wrong), maintaining that, at the scale of entire populations, the standard deviations σ_P^2 and σ_Q^2 are equal.

– The second step depends on the result of the first. Let us say:

S_x^2 = the square of the standard deviation of premiums observed in the first sample;

S_Y^2 = the square of the standard deviation of premiums observed in the second sample;

m_P = the average of premiums over the entirety of operations from which the first sample is taken;

m_q = the variance of premiums over the entirety of operations from which the second sample is taken;

$\bar{X}$ = average of premiums from the first sample;

$\bar{Y}$ = average of premiums from the second sample;

n_P = size of the first sample;

n_Q = size of the second sample.

- In the hypothesis where the two standard deviations are equal, the comparison test of the averages of two samples is characterized by the property by which variable T follows a Student law at $n_P + n_Q - 2$ degrees of freedom (Student test). That is:

$$T = \frac{\bar{X} - \bar{Y} - (m_P - m_Q)}{\sqrt{\frac{(n_P - 1)S_X^2 + (n_Q - 1)S_Y^2}{n_P + n_Q - 2}}\sqrt{\frac{1}{n_P} + \frac{1}{n_Q}}} \qquad [A23.4]$$

Thus, following the hypothesis $m_P = m_Q$, $T_0 = \frac{\bar{X}-\bar{Y}}{\sqrt{\frac{(n_P-1)S_X^2+(n_Q-1)S_Y^2}{n_P+n_Q-2}}\sqrt{\frac{1}{n_P}+\frac{1}{n_Q}}}$ follows a Student law at $n_P + n_Q - 2$ degrees of freedom, we calculate for the samples:

$$t_0 = \frac{\bar{X}-\bar{Y}}{\sqrt{\frac{(n_P-1)S_X^2+(n_Q-1)S_Y^2}{n_P+n_Q-2}}\sqrt{\frac{1}{n_P}+\frac{1}{n_Q}}} \qquad [A23.5]$$

Furthermore, it is possible to determine the value of the real c such that:

$$P[-c < T < c] = 1 - \alpha \qquad [A23.6]$$

where T is a Student variable. In this case:

$$c = F^{-1}\left(1 - \frac{\alpha}{2}\right) \qquad [A23.7]$$

where F is the distribution function of the Student law. Thus, for a level of confidence of 95%, $\alpha = 5\%$ and $c = F^{-1}\left(1 - \frac{0.05}{2}\right) = F^{-1}(0.975)$ obtained from the Student law table. Consequently, if $-c < t_0 < c$, the equality hypothesis of means can be accepted with an error risk of 5%. Inversely, if $t_0 > c$ or if $t_0 < -c$, the averages can be considered as significantly different with an error risk of 5%.

- If the unknown standard deviations are different, it is possible to use the Aspin–Welch test to find out if the averages of samples chosen are significantly different. In this case, following the equality hypothesis of means, the property for which variable $T = \frac{S_X^2}{S_Y^2} \cdot \frac{\sigma_Q^2}{\sigma_P^2}$ obeys the Fisher–Snedecor law with the parameters $n_P - 1$ and $n_Q - 1$, supposing that:

S_X^2 = the variance of the variable from the first sample;

S_Y^2 = the variance of the variable from the second sample;

σ_P^2 = the standard deviation of the variable for companies in the first sample;

σ_Q^2 = the standard deviation of the variable for companies in the second sample;

n_P = size of the first sample;

n_Q = size of the second sample.

- And:

$$\sigma_P^2 = \sigma_Q^2,\ T_0 = \frac{S_X^2}{S_Y^2} \text{ obeys } F(n_P - 1, n_Q - 1)$$

The number t_0 that satisfies $t_0 = \frac{S_X^2}{S_Y^2}$ can be determined using the samples. The Fisher–Snedecor table gives the value of c such that P[T > c] = 5%, where T obeys the law $F(m,n)$. Thus, if $t_0 > c$, the equality hypothesis of standard deviations must be rejected with a 5% chance of being wrong. Let us say:

$$T' = \frac{\overline{X} - \overline{Y} - (m_P - m_Q)}{\sqrt{\frac{(n_P-1)S_X^2 + (n_Q-1)S_Y^2}{n_P + n_Q - 2}}\sqrt{\frac{1}{n_P} + \frac{1}{n_Q}}} \qquad \text{[A23.8]}$$

which obeys a Student law with $n_P + n_Q - 2$ degrees of freedom. Thus, supposing $m_P = m_Q$,

$$T' = \frac{\overline{X} - \overline{Y}}{\sqrt{\frac{(n_P-1)S_X^2 + (n_Q-1)S_Y^2}{n_P + n_Q - 2}}\sqrt{\frac{1}{n_P} + \frac{1}{n_Q}}} \qquad \text{[A23.9]}$$

obeys a Student law with $n_P + n_Q - 2$ degrees of freedom. The number

$$t_0{}' = \frac{\overline{X} - \overline{Y}}{\sqrt{\frac{(n_P-1)S_X^2 + (n_Q-1)S_Y^2}{n_P + n_Q - 2}}\sqrt{\frac{1}{n_P} + \frac{1}{n_Q}}} \qquad \text{[A23.10]}$$

can be calculated through testing. It is also possible to calculate the value of c such that P[- c < T < c] = 1 – α, hence: $c = F^{-1}\left(1 - \frac{\alpha}{2}\right)$, where F is the distribution function for the Student law. Thus, with a 95% chance of being right, α = 5% and $c = F^{-1}(0.975)$, which can be obtained directly thanks to the Student law table. Consequently, if $-c < t_0 < c$, the equality hypothesis of means can be accepted with a 5% chance of error. If the standard deviations are different, an Aspin–Welch test must be done. Let us say $T = \frac{\bar{X}-\bar{Y}}{\sqrt{\frac{s_X^2}{n_P}+\frac{s_Y^2}{n_Q}}}$, which obeys the Student law with n degrees of freedom, where:

$$n = \frac{\left(\frac{s_X^2}{n_P}+\frac{s_Y^2}{n_Q}\right)^2}{\frac{\left(\frac{s_X^2}{n_P}\right)^2}{(n_P-1)}+\frac{\left(\frac{s_Y^2}{n_Q}\right)^2}{(n_Q-1)}} \qquad [A23.11]$$

The rule for the decision is the same as that of the Student test.

Bibliography

Research articles

Acharya, V., Gale, D., Yorulmazer, T. (2011). Rollover risk and market freezes. *Journal of Finance*, 66(4), 1177–1209.

Amihud, Y. and Mendelson, H. (1986). Asset pricing and the bid-ask spread. *Journal of Financial Economics*, 17(2), 223–249.

Bellalah, M. (1999). Les biais des modèles d'options revisités. *Revue française de gestion*, 025–124, 94–100.

Bellalah, M. (2000). La structure du capital et les options : l'impact du coût d'information, de l'impôt sur les sociétés et du risque de défaut. Working paper, Université Paris-Dauphine, France.

Bellalah, M. (2016). Issues in real options with shadow costs of incomplete information and short sales. *The Journal of Economic Asymmetries*, 13, 45–56.

Bellalah, M. and Jacquillat, B. (1995). Options valuation with information costs: Theory and tests. *Financial Review*, 30(3), 617–635.

Benartzi, S., Michaely, R., Thaler, R. (1997). Do changes in dividends signal the future or the past? *Journal of Finance*, 52(3), 1007–1034.

Black, F. (1996). Dividend puzzle. *Journal of Portfolio Management*, special issue, 8–12.

Black, F. and Cox, J. (1976). Valuing corporate securities: Some effects of bond indenture provisions. *Journal of Finance*, 31(2), 351–367.

Black, F. and Scholes, M. (1973). The pricing of options and corporate liabilities. *Journal of Political Economy*, 81(3), 637–654.

Bolton, P. and Scharfstein, D. (1996). Optimal debt structure and the number of creditors. *Journal of Political Economy*, 104(1), 1–25.

Boness, J.A. (1964). Elements of a theory of stock-option value. *Journal of Political Economy*, 72(2), 163–175.

Brennan, J. and Schwartz, E.S. (1978). Corporate income taxes, valuation and the problem of optimal capital structure. *Journal of Business*, 51(1), 103–114.

Campbell, J. and Taksler, G. (2003). Equity volatility and corporate bond yields. *Journal of Finance*, 58(6), 2321–2349.

Charitou, A. and Trigeorgis, L. (2004). Explaining bankruptcy using option theory [Online]. Available at: https://papers.ssrn.com/sol3/papers.cfm?abstract_id=675704.

Chava, S. and Roberts, M.R. (2008). How does financing impact investment? The role of debt covenants. *Journal of Finance*, 63(5), 2085–2121.

Chen, L., Lesmond, D., Wei, J. (2007). Corporate yield spreads and bond liquidity. *Journal of Finance*, 62(1), 119–149.

Cox, J., Ross, S., Rubinstein, M. (1979). Options pricing: A simplified approach. *Journal of Financial Economics*, 7(3), 229–263.

Deangelo, H., Deangelo, L., Skinner, D.J. (1992). Dividends and losses. *Journal of Finance*, 47(5), 1837–1863.

Diamond, D. (1989). Reputation acquisition in debt markets. *Journal of Political Economy*, 97(4), 828–862.

Elton, E., Gruber, M., Agrawal, D., Mann, C. (2001). Explaining the rate spread on corporate bonds. *Journal of Finance*, 56(1), 247–277.

Francois, P. and Morellec, E. (2004). Capital structure and asset prices: Some effects of bankruptcy procedures. *Journal of Business*, 77(2), 387–411.

Galaï, D. (1978). On the Boness and Black–Scholes models for valuation of call options. *Journal of Financial and Quantitative Analysis*, 13(1), 15–23.

Galaï, D. and Masulis, R.W. (1976). The option pricing model and the risk factor on stock. *Journal of Financial Economics*, 3(1/2), 53–81.

Galaï, D. and Wiener, Z. (2013). The impact of dividend policy on the valuation of equity, debt and credit risk. Research paper, The Hebrew University of Jerusalem, Israel.

Geske, R. (1977). The valuation of corporate liabilities. *Journal of Financial and Quantitative Analysis*, 12(4), 541–552.

Geske, R. (1979). The valuation of compound options. *Journal of Financial Economics*, 7(1), 63–81.

Geske, R. and Johnson, H. (1982). The valuation of corporate liabilities as compound options: A correction. *Journal of Financial and Quantitative Analysis*, 19(21), 231–232.

Gopalakrishnan, V. and Parkash, M. (1995). Borrower and lender perceptions of accounting information in corporate lending agreements. *Accounting Horizons*, 9(1), 13–26.

Gordon, R.D. (1941). Values of Mill's ratio of area to bounding ordinate and of the normal probability integral for large values of the arguments. *Annals of Mathematical Statistics*, 12, 364–366.

He, Z. and Xiong, W. (2012). Rollover risk and credit risk. *Journal of Finance*, 67(2), 391–430.

Heller, D. and Levyne, O. (2014). Is the growth potential of stock prices underestimated? *International Journal of Business*, 19(4), 336–360.

Heller, D. and Levyne, O. (2016). Cinema industry: Usefulness of the real options approach for valuation purpose. *International Journal of Business*, 21(1), 26–41.

Huang, J. and Huang, M. (2003). How much of corporate-treasury yield spread is due to credit risk? A new calibration approach. Working Paper, Penn State University, PA.

Hull, J.C., Nelken, I., White, A. (2005). Merton's model, credit risk and volatility skews. *Journal of Credit Risk*, 1(1), 3–28.

Jensen, M. and Long, J. (1972). Corporate investment under uncertainty and Pareto optimality in the capital markets. *Bell Journal of Economics and Management Science*, 3(1), 151–174.

Jensen, M.C. and Meckling, W.H. (1976). Theory of the firm: Managerial behavior, agency costs and capital structure. *Journal of Financial Economics*, 3(4), 305–360.

Jensen, M.C. and Meckling, W.H. (1979). Rights and production functions: An application to labor-managed firms and codetermination. *Journal of Business*, 52(4), 469–506.

Jones, E.P., Mason, S.P., Rosenfeld D. (1985). Contingent claims valuation of corporate liabilities: Theory and empirical test. In *Corporate Capital Structure in the United States*, Friedman, B.M. (ed.). University of Chicago Press, Chicago, IL.

Kalay, A. (1980). Signaling, information content, and the reluctance to cut dividends. *Journal of Financial and Quantitative Analysis*, 15(4), 855–873.

Kalay, A. (1982). Stockholder–bondholder conflict and dividend constraints. *Journal of Financial Economics*, 10(2), 211–233.

Kraus, A. and Litzenberger, R.H. (1973). A state preference model of optimal financing leverage. *Journal of Finance*, 28(4), 911–922.

Krishnamurthy, A. (2010). How debt markets have malfunctioned in the crisis. *Journal of Economic Perspectives*, 24(1), 3–28.

Leland, H.E. (1985). Option pricing and replication with transaction costs. *The Journal of Finance*, 40(5), 1283–1301.

Leland, H.E. (1994). Corporate debt value, bond covenants, and optimal capital structure. *Journal of Finance*, 49(4), 1213–1252.

Leland, H.E. (2004). Predictions of expected default probabilities in structural models of debt. *Journal of Investment Management*, 2(2), 5–20.

Leland, H.E. and Toft, K. (1996). Optimal capital structure, endogenous bankruptcy, and the term structure on credit spreads. *Journal of Finance*, 51(4), 987–1019.

Mello, A.S. and Parsons, J.E. (1992). Measuring the agency costs of debt. *Journal of Finance*, 47(5), 1887–1904.

Merton, R.C. (1971). Optimum consumption and portfolio rules in a continuous-time model. *Journal of Economic Theory*, 3(4), 373–413.

Merton, R.C. (1973). Theory of rational option pricing. *Bell Journal of Economics*, 4(1), 141–183.

Merton, R.C. (1974). On the pricing of corporate debt: The risk structure of interest rates. *Journal of Finance*, 29(2), 449–470.

Merton, R.C. (1987). A simple model of capital market equilibrium with incomplete information. *Journal of Finance*, 42(3), 483–510.

Merton, R.C and Subrahmanyam, M. (1974). The optimality of a competitive stock market. *Bell Journal of Economics and Management Science*, 5(1), 145–170.

Modigliani, F. and Miller, M.H. (1963). Taxes and the cost of capital: A correction. *American Economic Review*, 53(1), 433–443.

Morellec, E., Nikolov, B., Schürhoff, N. (2012). Corporate governance and capital structure dynamics. *Journal of Finance*, 67(3), 803–848.

Myers, S.C. (1977). Determinants of corporate borrowing. *Journal of Financial Economics*, 5(2), 147–175.

Rubinstein, M.E. (1973). A mean variance synthesis of corporate financial theory. *Journal of Finance*, 28(1), 167–181.

Sharpe, W. (1976). Capital asset prices: A theory of market equilibrium under conditions of risk. *Journal of Finance*, 19(3), 425–442.

Smith, C. and Warner, J. (1979). On financial contracting: Analysis of bonds covenants. *Journal of Financial Economics*, 7(2), 117–161.

Vassalou, M. and Xing, Y. (2004). Default risk in equity returns. *Journal of Finance*, 59(2), 831–868.

Wu, C., Li, Q., Wei, K.C.J. (1996). Incomplete-information capital market equilibrium with heterogeneous expectations and short sale restrictions. *Review of Quantitative Finance and Accounting*, 7(2), 119–136.

Books

Cox, J. and Rubinstein, M. (1985). *Options Markets*. Prentice Hall Englewood Cliffs, NJ.

Dixit, A. and Pindyck, R. (1994). Chapter 5. In *Investment Under Uncertainty*. Princeton University Press, Princeton, NJ.

Heller, D. (2018). Valorisation d'entreprise : méthodes traditionnelles et approche innovante par les options réelles. In *Tradition et innovation : de l'opposition à la complémentarité*, Anido Freire, N. (ed.). L'Harmattan, Paris.

Levyne, O. and Sahut, J.M. (2008). *Options réelles*. Dunod.

Vernimmen, P. (2016). *Finance d'entreprise*. Dalloz.

Miscellaneous

Ait-Mokhtar, Y. (2008). Comment les mécanismes de protection peuvent affecter significativement le cours d'une action. *La Lettre Vernimmen.net*, 63, 1–4.

Vasicek, O. (1984). *Credit Valuation*. KMV Corporation, San Francisco, CA.

Index

Other titles from

ISTE

in

Innovation, Entrepreneurship and Management

2021

ARCADE Jacques
Strategic Engineering (Innovation and Technology Set – Volume 11)

BÉRANGER Jérôme, RIZOULIÈRES Roland
The Digital Revolution in Health (Health and Innovation Set – Volume 2)

BOBILLIER CHAUMON Marc-Eric
Digital Transformations in the Challenge of Activity and Work: Understanding and Supporting Technological Changes (Technological Changes and Human Resources Set – Volume 3)

BUCLET Nicolas
Territorial Ecology and Socio-ecological Transition (Smart Innovation Set – Volume 34)

DIMOTIKALIS Yannis, KARAGRIGORIOU Alex, PARPOULA Christina, SKIADIS Christos H
Applied Modeling Techniques and Data Analysis 1: Computational Data Analysis Methods and Tools (Big Data, Artificial Intelligence and Data Analysis Set - Volume 7)
Applied Modeling Techniques and Data Analysis 2: Financial, Demographic, Stochastic and Statistical Models and Methods (Big Data, Artificial Intelligence and Data Analysis Set – Volume 8)

DISPAS Christophe, KAYANAKIS Georges, SERVEL Nicolas, STRIUKOVA Ludmila
Innovation and Financial Markets (Innovation between Risk and Reward Set – Volume 7)

ENJOLRAS Manon
Innovation and Export: The Joint Challenge of the Small Company (Smart Innovation Set – Volume 37)

FLEURY Sylvain, RICHIR Simon
Immersive Technologies to Accelerate Innovation: How Virtual and Augmented Reality Enables the Co-Creation of Concepts (Smart Innovation Set – Volume 38)

GIORGINI Pierre
The Contributory Revolution (Innovation and Technology Set – Volume 13)

GOGLIN Christian
Emotions and Values in Equity Crowdfunding Investment Choices 2: Modeling and Empirical Study

GRENIER Corinne, OIRY Ewan
Altering Frontiers: Organizational Innovations in Healthcare (Health and Innovation Set – Volume 1)

GUERRIER Claudine
Security and Its Challenges in the 21st Century (Innovation and Technology Set – Volume 12)

HELLER David
Performance of Valuation Methods in Financial Transactions (Modern Finance, Management Innovation and Economic Growth Set – Volume 4)

LEHMANN Paul-Jacques
Liberalism and Capitalism Today

SOULÉ Bastien, HALLÉ Julie, VIGNAL Bénédicte, BOUTROY Éric, NIER Olivier
Innovation Trajectories and Process Optimization (Smart Innovation Set – Volume 35)

UZUNIDIS Dimitri, KASMI Fedoua, ADATTO Laurent
Innovation Economics, Engineering and Management Handbook 1: Main Themes
Innovation Economics, Engineering and Management Handbook 2: Special Themes

VALLIER Estelle
Innovation in Clusters: Science–Industry Relationships in the Face of Forced Advancement (Smart Innovation Set – Volume 36)

2020

ACH Yves-Alain, RMADI-SAÏD Sandra
Financial Information and Brand Value: Reflections, Challenges and Limitations

ANDREOSSO-O'CALLAGHAN Bernadette, DZEVER Sam, JAUSSAUD Jacques, TAYLOR Robert
Sustainable Development and Energy Transition in Europe and Asia (Innovation and Technology Set – Volume 9)

BEN SLIMANE Sonia, M'HENNI Hatem
Entrepreneurship and Development: Realities and Future Prospects (Smart Innovation Set – Volume 30)

CHOUTEAU Marianne, FOREST Joëlle, NGUYEN Céline
Innovation for Society: The P.S.I. Approach (Smart Innovation Set – Volume 28)

CORON Clotilde
Quantifying Human Resources: Uses and Analysis
(Technological Changes and Human Resources Set – Volume 2)

CORON Clotilde, GILBERT Patrick
Technological Change
(Technological Changes and Human Resources Set – Volume 1)

CERDIN Jean-Luc, PERETTI Jean-Marie
The Success of Apprenticeships: Views of Stakeholders on Training and Learning (Human Resources Management Set – Volume 3)

DELCHET-COCHET Karen
Circular Economy: From Waste Reduction to Value Creation
(Economic Growth Set – Volume 2)

DIDAY Edwin, GUAN Rong, SAPORTA Gilbert, WANG Huiwen
Advances in Data Science
(Big Data, Artificial Intelligence and Data Analysis Set – Volume 4)

DOS SANTOS PAULINO Victor
Innovation Trends in the Space Industry
(Smart Innovation Set – Volume 25)

GASMI Nacer
Corporate Innovation Strategies: Corporate Social Responsibility and Shared Value Creation
(Smart Innovation Set – Volume 33)

GOGLIN Christian
Emotions and Values in Equity Crowdfunding Investment Choices 1: Transdisciplinary Theoretical Approach

GUILHON Bernard
Venture Capital and the Financing of Innovation
(Innovation Between Risk and Reward Set – Volume 6)

LATOUCHE Pascal
Open Innovation: Human Set-up
(Innovation and Technology Set – Volume 10)

LIMA Marcos
Entrepreneurship and Innovation Education: Frameworks and Tools (Smart Innovation Set – Volume 32)

MACHADO Carolina, DAVIM J. Paulo
Sustainable Management for Managers and Engineers

MAKRIDES Andreas, KARAGRIGORIOU Alex, SKIADAS Christos H.
Data Analysis and Applications 3: Computational, Classification, Financial, Statistical and Stochastic Methods
(Big Data, Artificial Intelligence and Data Analysis Set – Volume 5)
Data Analysis and Applications 4: Financial Data Analysis and Methods
(Big Data, Artificial Intelligence and Data Analysis Set – Volume 6)

MASSOTTE Pierre, CORSI Patrick
Complex Decision-Making in Economy and Finance

MEUNIER François-Xavier
Dual Innovation Systems: Concepts, Tools and Methods (Smart Innovation Set – Volume 31)

MICHAUD Thomas
Science Fiction and Innovation Design (Innovation in Engineering and Technology Set – Volume 6)

MONINO Jean-Louis
Data Control: Major Challenge for the Digital Society (Smart Innovation Set – Volume 29)

MORLAT Clément
Sustainable Productive System: Eco-development versus Sustainable Development (Smart Innovation Set – Volume 26)

SAULAIS Pierre, ERMINE Jean-Louis
Knowledge Management in Innovative Companies 2: Understanding and Deploying a KM Plan within a Learning Organization (Smart Innovation Set – Volume 27)

2019

AMENDOLA Mario, GAFFARD Jean-Luc
Disorder and Public Concern Around Globalization

BARBAROUX Pierre
Disruptive Technology and Defence Innovation Ecosystems
(Innovation in Engineering and Technology Set – Volume 5)

DOU Henri, JUILLET Alain, CLERC Philippe
Strategic Intelligence for the Future 1: A New Strategic and Operational Approach
Strategic Intelligence for the Future 2: A New Information Function Approach

FRIKHA Azza
Measurement in Marketing: Operationalization of Latent Constructs

FRIMOUSSE Soufyane
Innovation and Agility in the Digital Age
(Human Resources Management Set – Volume 2)

GAY Claudine, SZOSTAK Bérangère L.
Innovation and Creativity in SMEs: Challenges, Evolutions and Prospects
(Smart Innovation Set – Volume 21)

GORIA Stéphane, HUMBERT Pierre, ROUSSEL Benoît
Information, Knowledge and Agile Creativity
(Smart Innovation Set – Volume 22)

HELLER David
Investment Decision-making Using Optional Models
(Economic Growth Set – Volume 2)

HELLER David, DE CHADIRAC Sylvain, HALAOUI Lana, JOUVET Camille
The Emergence of Start-ups
(Economic Growth Set – Volume 1)

HÉRAUD Jean-Alain, KERR Fiona, BURGER-HELMCHEN Thierry
Creative Management of Complex Systems
(Smart Innovation Set – Volume 19)

LATOUCHE Pascal
Open Innovation: Corporate Incubator
(Innovation and Technology Set – Volume 7)

LEHMANN Paul-Jacques
The Future of the Euro Currency

LEIGNEL Jean-Louis, MÉNAGER Emmanuel, YABLONSKY Serge
Sustainable Enterprise Performance: A Comprehensive Evaluation Method

LIÈVRE Pascal, AUBRY Monique, GAREL Gilles
Management of Extreme Situations: From Polar Expeditions to Exploration-Oriented Organizations

MILLOT Michel
Embarrassment of Product Choices 2: Towards a Society of Well-being

N'GOALA Gilles, PEZ-PÉRARD Virginie, PRIM-ALLAZ Isabelle
Augmented Customer Strategy: CRM in the Digital Age

NIKOLOVA Blagovesta
The RRI Challenge: Responsibilization in a State of Tension with Market Regulation
(Innovation and Responsibility Set – Volume 3)

PELLEGRIN-BOUCHER Estelle, ROY Pierre
Innovation in the Cultural and Creative Industries
(Innovation and Technology Set – Volume 8)

PRIOLON Joël
Financial Markets for Commodities

QUINIOU Matthieu
Blockchain: The Advent of Disintermediation

RAVIX Joël-Thomas, DESCHAMPS Marc
Innovation and Industrial Policies
(Innovation between Risk and Reward Set – Volume 5)

ROGER Alain, VINOT Didier
Skills Management: New Applications, New Questions
(Human Resources Management Set – Volume 1)

SAULAIS Pierre, ERMINE Jean-Louis
Knowledge Management in Innovative Companies 1: Understanding and Deploying a KM Plan within a Learning Organization
(Smart Innovation Set – Volume 23)

SERVAJEAN-HILST Romaric
Co-innovation Dynamics: The Management of Client-Supplier Interactions for Open Innovation
(Smart Innovation Set – Volume 20)

SKIADAS Christos H., BOZEMAN James R.
Data Analysis and Applications 1: Clustering and Regression, Modeling-estimating, Forecasting and Data Mining
(Big Data, Artificial Intelligence and Data Analysis Set – Volume 2)
Data Analysis and Applications 2: Utilization of Results in Europe and Other Topics
(Big Data, Artificial Intelligence and Data Analysis Set – Volume 3)

UZUNIDIS Dimitri
Systemic Innovation: Entrepreneurial Strategies and Market Dynamics

VIGEZZI Michel
World Industrialization: Shared Inventions, Competitive Innovations and Social Dynamics
(Smart Innovation Set – Volume 24)

2018

BURKHARDT Kirsten
Private Equity Firms: Their Role in the Formation of Strategic Alliances

CALLENS Stéphane
Creative Globalization
(Smart Innovation Set – Volume 16)

CASADELLA Vanessa
Innovation Systems in Emerging Economies: MINT – Mexico, Indonesia, Nigeria, Turkey
(Smart Innovation Set – Volume 18)

CHOUTEAU Marianne, FOREST Joëlle, NGUYEN Céline
Science, Technology and Innovation Culture
(Innovation in Engineering and Technology Set – Volume 3)

CORLOSQUET-HABART Marine, JANSSEN Jacques
Big Data for Insurance Companies
(Big Data, Artificial Intelligence and Data Analysis Set – Volume 1)

CROS Françoise
Innovation and Society
(Smart Innovation Set – Volume 15)

DEBREF Romain
Environmental Innovation and Ecodesign: Certainties and Controversies
(Smart Innovation Set – Volume 17)

DOMINGUEZ Noémie
SME Internationalization Strategies: Innovation to Conquer New Markets

ERMINE Jean-Louis
Knowledge Management: The Creative Loop
(Innovation and Technology Set – Volume 5)

GILBERT Patrick, BOBADILLA Natalia, GASTALDI Lise,
LE BOULAIRE Martine, LELEBINA Olga
Innovation, Research and Development Management

IBRAHIMI Mohammed
Mergers & Acquisitions: Theory, Strategy, Finance

LEMAÎTRE Denis
Training Engineers for Innovation

LÉVY Aldo, BEN BOUHENI Faten, AMMI Chantal
Financial Management: USGAAP and IFRS Standards
(Innovation and Technology Set – Volume 6)

MILLOT Michel
Embarrassment of Product Choices 1: How to Consume Differently

PANSERA Mario, OWEN Richard
Innovation and Development: The Politics at the Bottom of the Pyramid (Innovation and Responsibility Set – Volume 2)

RICHEZ Yves
Corporate Talent Detection and Development

SACHETTI Philippe, ZUPPINGER Thibaud
New Technologies and Branding
(Innovation and Technology Set – Volume 4)

SAMIER Henri
Intuition, Creativity, Innovation

TEMPLE Ludovic, COMPAORÉ SAWADOGO Eveline M.F.W.
Innovation Processes in Agro-Ecological Transitions in Developing Countries
(Innovation in Engineering and Technology Set – Volume 2)

UZUNIDIS Dimitri
Collective Innovation Processes: Principles and Practices
(Innovation in Engineering and Technology Set – Volume 4)

VAN HOOREBEKE Delphine
The Management of Living Beings or Emo-management

2017

AÏT-EL-HADJ Smaïl
The Ongoing Technological System
(Smart Innovation Set – Volume 11)

BAUDRY Marc, DUMONT Béatrice
Patents: Prompting or Restricting Innovation?
(Smart Innovation Set – Volume 12)

BÉRARD Céline, TEYSSIER Christine
Risk Management: Lever for SME Development and Stakeholder Value Creation

CHALENÇON Ludivine
Location Strategies and Value Creation of International Mergers and Acquisitions

CHAUVEL Danièle, BORZILLO Stefano
The Innovative Company: An Ill-defined Object
(Innovation between Risk and Reward Set – Volume 1)

CORSI Patrick
Going Past Limits To Growth

D'ANDRIA Aude, GABARRET Inés
Building 21st Century Entrepreneurship
(Innovation and Technology Set – Volume 2)

DAIDJ Nabyla
Cooperation, Coopetition and Innovation
(Innovation and Technology Set – Volume 3)

FERNEZ-WALCH Sandrine
The Multiple Facets of Innovation Project Management
(Innovation between Risk and Reward Set – Volume 4)

FOREST Joëlle
Creative Rationality and Innovation
(Smart Innovation Set – Volume 14)

GUILHON Bernard
Innovation and Production Ecosystems
(Innovation between Risk and Reward Set – Volume 2)

HAMMOUDI Abdelhakim, DAIDJ Nabyla
Game Theory Approach to Managerial Strategies and Value Creation
(Diverse and Global Perspectives on Value Creation Set – Volume 3)

LALLEMENT Rémi
Intellectual Property and Innovation Protection: New Practices and New Policy Issues
(Innovation between Risk and Reward Set – Volume 3)

LAPERCHE Blandine
Enterprise Knowledge Capital
(Smart Innovation Set – Volume 13)

LEBERT Didier, EL YOUNSI Hafida
International Specialization Dynamics
(Smart Innovation Set – Volume 9)

MAESSCHALCK Marc
Reflexive Governance for Research and Innovative Knowledge
(Responsible Research and Innovation Set – Volume 6)

MASSOTTE Pierre
Ethics in Social Networking and Business 1: Theory, Practice and Current Recommendations
Ethics in Social Networking and Business 2: The Future and Changing Paradigms

MASSOTTE Pierre, CORSI Patrick
Smart Decisions in Complex Systems

MEDINA Mercedes, HERRERO Mónica, URGELLÉS Alicia
Current and Emerging Issues in the Audiovisual Industry
(Diverse and Global Perspectives on Value Creation Set – Volume 1)

MICHAUD Thomas
Innovation, Between Science and Science Fiction
(Smart Innovation Set – Volume 10)

PELLÉ Sophie
Business, Innovation and Responsibility
(Responsible Research and Innovation Set – Volume 7)

SAVIGNAC Emmanuelle
The Gamification of Work: The Use of Games in the Workplace

SUGAHARA Satoshi, DAIDJ Nabyla, USHIO Sumitaka
Value Creation in Management Accounting and Strategic Management: An Integrated Approach
(Diverse and Global Perspectives on Value Creation Set –Volume 2)

UZUNIDIS Dimitri, SAULAIS Pierre
Innovation Engines: Entrepreneurs and Enterprises in a Turbulent World (Innovation in Engineering and Technology Set – Volume 1)

2016

BARBAROUX Pierre, ATTOUR Amel, SCHENK Eric
Knowledge Management and Innovation (Smart Innovation Set – Volume 6)

BEN BOUHENI Faten, AMMI Chantal, LEVY Aldo
Banking Governance, Performance And Risk-Taking: Conventional Banks Vs Islamic Banks

BOUTILLIER Sophie, CARRÉ Denis, LEVRATTO Nadine
Entrepreneurial Ecosystems (Smart Innovation Set – Volume 2)

BOUTILLIER Sophie, UZUNIDIS Dimitri
The Entrepreneur (Smart Innovation Set – Volume 8)

BOUVARD Patricia, SUZANNE Hervé
Collective Intelligence Development in Business

GALLAUD Delphine, LAPERCHE Blandine
Circular Economy, Industrial Ecology and Short Supply Chains (Smart Innovation Set – Volume 4)

GUERRIER Claudine
Security and Privacy in the Digital Era (Innovation and Technology Set – Volume 1)

MEGHOUAR Hicham
Corporate Takeover Targets

MONINO Jean-Louis, SEDKAOUI Soraya
Big Data, Open Data and Data Development (Smart Innovation Set – Volume 3)

MOREL Laure, LE ROUX Serge
Fab Labs: Innovative User (Smart Innovation Set – Volume 5)

PICARD Fabienne, TANGUY Corinne
Innovations and Techno-ecological Transition
(Smart Innovation Set – Volume 7)

2015

CASADELLA Vanessa, LIU Zeting, DIMITRI Uzunidis
Innovation Capabilities and Economic Development in Open Economies
(Smart Innovation Set – Volume 1)

CORSI Patrick, MORIN Dominique
Sequencing Apple's DNA

CORSI Patrick, NEAU Erwan
Innovation Capability Maturity Model

FAIVRE-TAVIGNOT Bénédicte
Social Business and Base of the Pyramid

GODÉ Cécile
Team Coordination in Extreme Environments

MAILLARD Pierre
Competitive Quality and Innovation

MASSOTTE Pierre, CORSI Patrick
Operationalizing Sustainability

MASSOTTE Pierre, CORSI Patrick
Sustainability Calling

2014

DUBÉ Jean, LEGROS Diègo
Spatial Econometrics Using Microdata

LESCA Humbert, LESCA Nicolas
Strategic Decisions and Weak Signals

2013

HABART-CORLOSQUET Marine, JANSSEN Jacques, MANCA Raimondo
VaR Methodology for Non-Gaussian Finance

2012

DAL PONT Jean-Pierre
Process Engineering and Industrial Management

MAILLARD Pierre
Competitive Quality Strategies

POMEROL Jean-Charles
Decision-Making and Action

SZYLAR Christian
UCITS Handbook

2011

LESCA Nicolas
Environmental Scanning and Sustainable Development

LESCA Nicolas, LESCA Humbert
Weak Signals for Strategic Intelligence: Anticipation Tool for Managers

MERCIER-LAURENT Eunika
Innovation Ecosystems

2010

SZYLAR Christian
Risk Management under UCITS III/IV

2009

COHEN Corine
Business Intelligence

ZANINETTI Jean-Marc
Sustainable Development in the USA

2008

CORSI Patrick, DULIEU Mike
The Marketing of Technology Intensive Products and Services

DZEVER Sam, JAUSSAUD Jacques, ANDREOSSO Bernadette
Evolving Corporate Structures and Cultures in Asia: Impact of Globalization

2007

AMMI Chantal
Global Consumer Behavior

2006

BOUGHZALA Imed, ERMINE Jean-Louis
Trends in Enterprise Knowledge Management

CORSI Patrick *et al.*
Innovation Engineering: the Power of Intangible Networks

Printed and bound by CPI Group (UK) Ltd, Croydon, CR0 4YY
13/09/2026
14961037-0001